GOOD AND BAD TASTE

GOOD AND BAD TASTE

by

ODD BROCHMANN

Translated from
the Norwegian by
M. A. MICHAEL

EYRE & SPOTTISWOODE · LONDON · 1955

The translator wishes to record his
gratitude to Mr. Alan Lindsay, A.R.C.A.,
for vetting his text and for his many
valuable suggestions

The original edition, 'Om Stygt og Pent',
was first published in Oslo in 1953

The first English edition 1955

This book is printed in Great Britain
for Eyre & Spottiswoode (Publishers) Ltd., 15 Bedford Street,
London, W.C.2, by Jarrold & Sons Ltd., Norwich

CONTENTS

CHAPTER ONE

Which explains for whom the book was written, why it was written, and how careful you have to be about forming opinions.

This book deals with *things*, all the things which people make for their adornment, their comfort or their use, with their nature and manifold properties. It attempts to explain what it is that determines our ideas about them, why some of them seem to us to be ugly, while others are more attractive, perhaps even seem beautiful. And by *things* is here meant every possible kind of thing, ranging from jewellery or the tools which we take in our hands, to furniture and dwellings and whole buildings. Then we shall turn our attention to the effect things have when they are combined in different ways, as for example, when we put furniture into a room.

From this it can be seen for whom the book was written: that is for all those who have to do, or who will have to do with these things. In the first place this means those who have thought of becoming architects or designers for industry, or craftsmen. But not only for those. In practice almost everybody has to deal with things: one embroiders cloth and someone else can make a lampshade at a pinch. And *everybody* is sooner or later compelled to make a choice between the millions of things there are, if only when they set up house for themselves. Then they must first discover what they like and need, and afterwards assemble it in such a way that the final result really conforms to their inmost

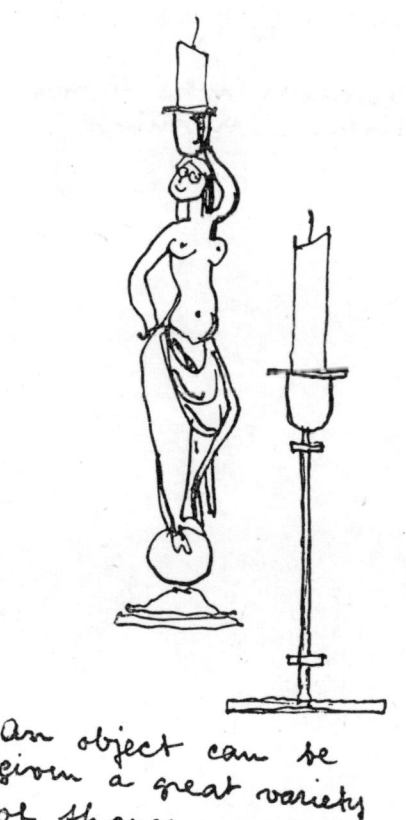

An object can be given a great variety of shapes and forms.

Someone who knows
their own mind.

conception of how it should all be. Thus you can say that this book was really written for everybody.

This business of *knowing* about the properties of everyday things is most necessary, for our immediate reaction to them is often based on the most fortuitous impulses, even when we are most sure of ourselves.

Let us imagine someone who is very dogmatic, a domineering woman at an exhibition of furniture, who walks round expressing her opinion of the exhibits in pithy, forceful language. "That lamp there," she perhaps says, "is ugly. But the shade is quite lovely. The table in the corner isn't so bad, but never in all my born days have I seen anything as ghastly as that cupboard."

Now, it is reasonable to suppose that all the things she mentioned were made by people who had some purpose in making what they did, and who no doubt considered that they had achieved things of beauty. Their ideas need not necessarily be right, but the fact that they had them is sufficient to make us curious. Who is right, and why? It will thus be natural to ask the lady how she can know all the things she said.

Her answer would probably be: "Know? That isn't a thing you need to *know*; it is what I think and that's all there is to it."

But it isn't. There is so much more to it that we have made a whole book about it. Not that we want to think the same about all things, but just to discover why we think what we do. We may like a piece of furniture because it reminds us of grandfather's home and the lovely summer holidays we used to spend there, or we may like a chair because we know from personal experience that it is comfortable to sit in. We may think the shape itself is attractive, even though we may never have seen anything like it before. In that latter case it must be because it harmonizes with something inside us, gives us an agreeable feeling which must coincide with other kinds of feelings we have. Or we can experience a disagreeable sensation from what is in itself a good thing, merely because it is new and therefore startling. We have an oppressive feeling that we have to put ourselves into a certain way of thinking if we are to be able to accept it (and that is a thing of which most of us instinctively fight shy). But not till we are to a certain extent able to survey all these facts will we be entitled to express an opinion, even to ourselves. Then, too, you will find it easier to talk with others about these things than at first you would have thought: this business of *taste* is not so incalculable as it is often supposed to be.

The knowledge that we acquire by doing this will make us in many ways more fastidious, but that is all to the good. On the other hand it will also make us more understanding. Together, this means that we shall become the richer, be able to understand more; have the pleasure which always accompanies knowledge of matters and things.

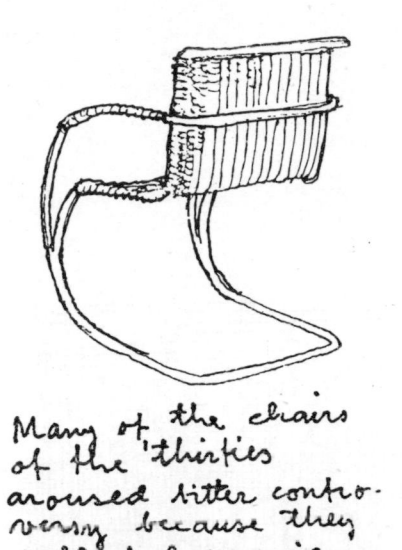

Many of the chairs of the 'thirties aroused bitter controversy because they reflected new ideas.

It must be admitted that those who gruffly remark that this question of taste and liking is not a thing which can be discussed have a certain amount of justification on their side. A grown man can maintain that a fillet steak is the nicest thing to eat, while a little girl will think that trifle is. Neither is to be reproached for thinking so. But if the man we are speaking of refuses to eat trifle, then we are justified in saying that he is poorer by one pleasure than he who enjoys both, though he may still prefer one to the other. And he who cannot distinguish between what is well and badly made is generally held to have no right to express an opinion at all.

We like people who know about things, who know what they are talking about. And when dealing with things like houses and furniture, we must almost demand that people be possessed of a certain insight, because those are important things which concern us all. It is decisive for the well-being both of ourselves and of others, since we have to associate one with another. We all live in a community built up on a sense of co-operation and fellowship.

OUR CONSCIOUSNESS OF SPACE IN EVERYTHING

We all need to feel that we can live in the place which we inhabit, that we can live happily in our homes and among the things we collect around us. It is natural to start by asking: Are there any definite rules as to how a room should be shaped if people are to be able to feel they can live there, nature having made us what we are? The easiest way to answer this is, perhaps, to put the question the other way round. Let us see if we can imagine a room in which we definitely could *not* live or be happy, no matter what our tastes, habits or circumstances might be. That sounds easy enough, but just to be sure, let us give some simple examples.

A room with bare walls painted black, with almost no window space and sparsely furnished with furniture of iron painted black, would not appear attractive to anyone. We would all agree in calling it gloomy and cheerless and a place in which we could not live. Next, let us imagine a room which is light and friendly enough, but its walls are hung with black draperies and the floor is crowded with heavy over-upholstered furniture stuffed with big silk cushions and on the tables are embroidered runners with fringes. A few people might like the room, because its furnishings bear witness to prosperity, but most of us would find it impossible to live in because we would not have room to move, we would feel imprisoned. In either case our reaction is due to a feeling of not being able to do in such surroundings the things that we normally like to do.

But we can also imagine rooms which satisfy all our requirements for light, colour and furnishing, both for

Would you feel at home here?

Or here?

repose and for doing things: yet if we make such a room with a ceiling thirty feet high (assuming it to be an ordinary room we are dealing with) we should find that we wouldn't be able to live in that either. We should feel as though we were at the bottom of a shaft; we should feel strangely small and lost with all that air above us. So, let us lower the ceiling to just above our heads. That isn't right, either. Even though we can stand upright perfectly well we say that we feel oppressed, and that we can't breathe, though there is really lots of air all round us. In both these cases it is the *shape* of the room, in relation to ourselves, which is wrong.

Uncomfortable,

Now suppose we make a room with the ceiling at the normal height, but with walls which have violent bulges in them. We should find ourselves seriously uncomfortable; it is as though the whole room were in motion so that we become quite seasick. Yet everything is in fact stable and fixed, it is only that our *eye* is without points of fixture and so wanders uncertainly hither and thither.

Finally, suppose we fashion a room as pleasant and normal as it can be so far as size and proportions go, but with the walls made of heavy, squared blocks of stone. We shouldn't like this room either; we should think that it is heavy and hard, or violent in character. We use those words about it, yet it would not have occurred to us to do so if the walls had been of concrete painted red, though concrete is just as heavy and hard as stone.

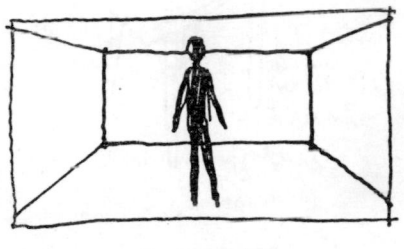

uncomfortable,

All these rooms we have made, we can furnish just as we like; there is no interference of any kind. We can walk upright in the low room, and we don't need to touch the rugged stone walls. It may therefore seem at first that we haven't any right to call these rooms ugly or un-pleasant, yet none the less they make a bad impression. That is because we feel as though we were lost at the bottom of a shaft, as though we really might bang our heads on the low ceiling, as though we were in a rough sea with those

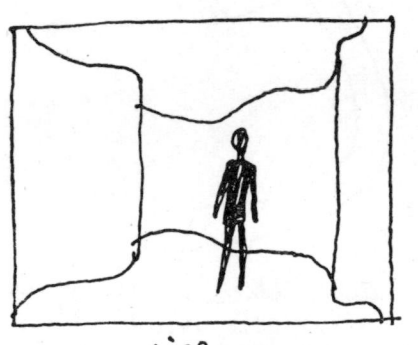

and still more uncomfortable.

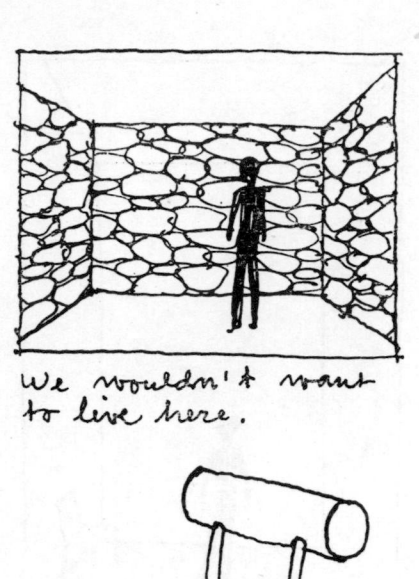

We wouldn't want to live here.

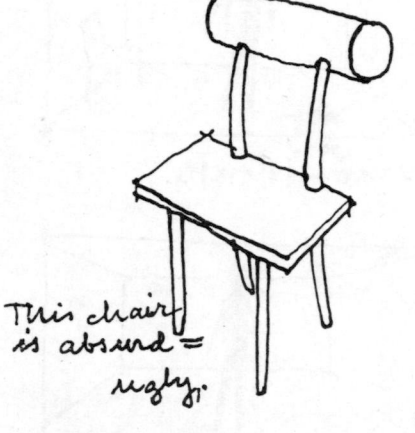

This chair is absurd = ugly.

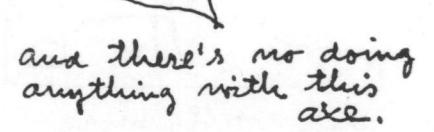

and there's no doing anything with this axe.

curved walls, or as though we could not avoid coming up against the hard stone. That is what we think, whether we wish it or not, and thus we let the shape affect us.

In the margin is the drawing of a chair which will appear unusual to most of us. Our immediate reaction is to call it ugly, and there we are right because it is impossible to sit on. It has an ugly shape–as a chair. It is again with the shape we are concerned when we come to judge the peculiar axe drawn beneath the chair. You don't need to be a professional lumberjack to see that that is a dangerous implement, and therefore it hurts even to look at it.

In all these examples, which are so simple and which yet deal with decisive qualities in the things we are continually coming up against, we have had to use the word shape or *form* to explain what we are talking about. When dealing with the chair and the axe we had experience to go by, with the different rooms it was merely a matter of sensation, but the sensation is inescapable. What then is this strange and complicated concept of form or shape? Before we can get anywhere, we must examine it a little more closely.

CHAPTER TWO

Which deals with that strange and complicated thing we call form, or shape, considered as a thing by itself.

ORDER AND CONFUSION

In one way we can say that the concept of form is a thing which goes with man's desire for *order*. This sense of order is itself something which man has developed so as to emphasize that he is a thinking creature and not just at the mercy of chance. With it we can show that we are in a position both to register things and to control them.

The drawing in the margin depicts a heap of stones piled up in a haphazard, we could almost say in a *muddled*, way. By that we mean that the form of the heap is not easy to distinguish, nor, by running our eye over it, can we so easily say how many stones there are there. We can make an experiment to illustrate this, by shutting the book and trying to draw what we have just seen. It is highly improbable that our drawing will be anything like correct, either as regards the arrangement of the stones or their number. That is what makes us call the drawing chaotic. *It has no shape or form which is easy to grasp.*

Now let us put the stones in some sort of order; for example, arranging them as shown in the next drawing. At once our mind, our eye, has got something to go on, a point of fixture, the whole thing has acquired a significant shape or pattern. Some will say perhaps that it has been given the shape of a star, others that it forms a ring round a central point. In actual fact it hasn't either of those shapes; it is our

Disorder = lack of form.

Order = Form

Different order —
different form

Muddle

eye which has been at work drawing invisible criss-cross lines through the centre or in a ring through the outer parts. If we now shut the book again, we will have a far better chance of recording what we have seen, both as regards the number and the relative positions of the stones.

It will perhaps make this point even clearer if we arrange the stones in a square, three along each side and one in the middle (or in three rows of three, if we prefer to look at it that way). It is now easy to explain and reproduce the form accurately, and as far as the number of the stones is concerned, no doubt is possible: it is $3 \times 3 = 9$.

The remarkable thing about the shapes and forms we have made here, is that they are so easily comprehended, so clearly discernible, and yet they do not represent anything we know from Nature. (It is true that we used the term star for one of them, but stars don't look like that.) That we nevertheless find them so easy to grasp is because we *know* something about them. We don't need a wonderful education to recognize a circle and a square, and to know that those are forms which man has discovered and which are governed by certain laws. We know these laws, and most people today take them as a mere matter of course and no longer think about them. Therefore we have now established as a fact what was said in the introduction, that our appreciation of form is *based on our knowledge of and acquaintance with things.*

Now let us see how our first reaction agrees with our consciousness of form and shape in daily life. The drawing in the margin depicts what might be a desk with a lot of things lying on it higgledy-piggledy. If we (or many of us) find the sight unpleasant, it is not because our mothers brought us up to be tidy, nor because we are pernickety by nature. We don't like it, because we cannot see properly what is on the table, and because our eye has no point of focus and must roam about restlessly.

In the next drawing someone has been at the table and tidied it. Whoever did so was probably activated by just the ordinary sense of order, but subconsciously he was moved by a deeper urge for form. The things have not been arranged in any geometrical pattern, but, all the same, we find it easier to see both the whole and the individual articles. It is easier to find what you want, is what we tell people when urging them to be tidy. Of course it is. But why have the articles been assembled in just that way? In the drawing below they have been arranged quite differently. This introduces something which is more difficult to find out about, perceptions which are linked with concepts of different kinds, and which are governed by forces that we shall be discussing later.

and order.

When we furnish our rooms, we do so in accordance with the same rules. We arrange things so that they form groups or distinct systems. Yet of all the possibilities which are always open to us, those we choose are the ones which will also satisfy our intuitive requirements in another way, whether these are for utility or by virtue of other considerations which necessitate special attention.

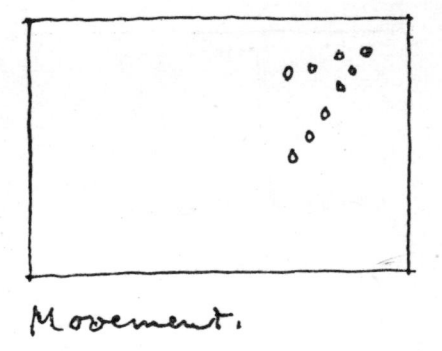

THE SENSATION OF MOVEMENT

Let us go back to the nine stones we instanced earlier and place them on the top of a table. (But now we must look at them from farther away.) All at once, it looks as though they were just about to move over the edge, to be more exact, into the top right-hand corner. In reality, of course, they are not moving at all. This is a queer phenomenon which is of particular importance in sculpture. In certain arrangements points and lines on a picture surface can give the impression that they are leading a life of their own, of being in motion. In this way it is possible for the painter or sculptor to produce the effect of

Movement.

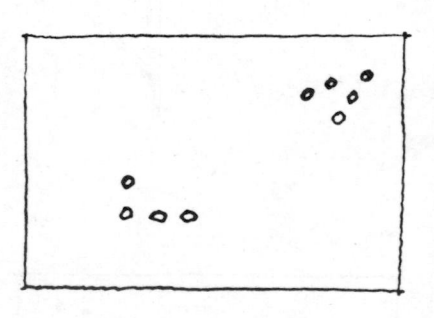

rest

and tension.

something in motion, something which is happening, without employing examples from Nature which represent those things (for example, a bird in flight). Or, if he first paints a flying bird, he can so place it in the picture, and surround it with such lines that the feeling of movement is enhanced.

We are not concerned with pictorial art, but with more utilitarian things. And we don't like it if these give the impression of wanting to fly off. On the contrary, with our conceptions of pleasant surroundings, we can even say that the aim of all architecture and decoration has always been to establish a feeling of rest and repose, though with certain reservations. But let us first go a step further with our experiments.

If we arrange our stones in a square in the middle of the table we get a definite feeling of restfulness. We say that the picture is static (in equilibrium). Arranged in the shape of a snow-plough up in the corner, the stones give the impression of something in motion, and we then say that the picture is *dynamic* (which actually means: in motion as the result of forces). But if we arrange them as two snow-ploughs each ploughing its own way, then there is rest again, provided the forces appear to us to be of equal strength. However, the rest achieved in this way is somehow more tense than the first; we have a feeling that there is a continual struggle going on between the two groups. We like to say then that the groups keep each other in a state of *tension*, that an element of tension has been introduced into the picture.

Now we can let our personal taste and ideas have a say. Which do we like best: the form of rest which is quite static, or that in which there is tension? It is obvious that opinions will vary here both with individuals and with the age. Some people are more cautious and cool in their attitude, while others want things to be a bit more forcible.

We must again try to put what we know into practice, and we can begin with a thing like hanging pictures on a

16

wall. One way you often see, is the pictures hanging step-wise along a slanting line. That, however, is not a good arrangement, since we immediately get the impression of movement, and the effect of that is unpleasant where a wall is concerned. We prefer a wall to appear fixed and solid, and so give us a feeling of security. There is also another thing that happens: whether we like it or not, our eye will draw an oblique line through the pictures and thereby the wall will be divided diagonally, a division which appears meaningless in relation to the horizontal and vertical lines which dominate most rooms.

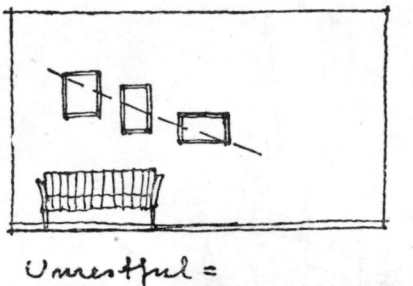

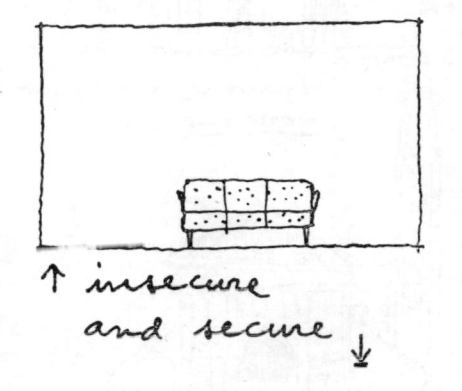

Unrestful = ugly way of hanging pictures.

A sofa placed haphazard on a long wall can give us a similar impression of wanting to sail off on its own; but as soon as it comes near one of the corners it will seem to be standing firmly again. The same is true when it stands in the middle of the wall, for then it will be fixed by an invisible tie to a centre line which is also invisible, but which we intuitively recognize. But it is also possible to introduce new elements which 'fix' the sofa in its position. You can put a table in front of it, or one or two chairs on the other side which will act as an anchor in conjunction with the floor or other groups of furniture.

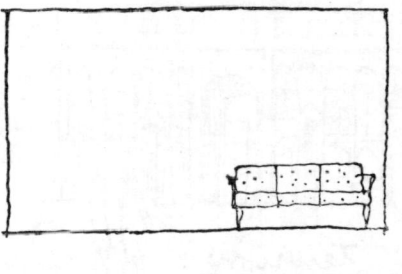

↑ insecure and secure ↓

It has been said that all appearance of movement is bad in architecture, but, strictly speaking, this is only true of movement in a horizontal or oblique direction, where there is nothing to stop the movement; it is not necessarily so where the motion is straight up or down. Imagine a low house with large roof surfaces with only a slight slope; the gable will then look as though the whole were being pressed downwards, into the ground. The effect of this can often be good; and we then say that the house lies well on the ground, and the whole impression is of something snug and secure, which is what we like, for example, in huts and houses in exposed places. We don't feel anxious, for we know that the ground is solid, that it, as it were, presses back.

Downward movement, pressure.

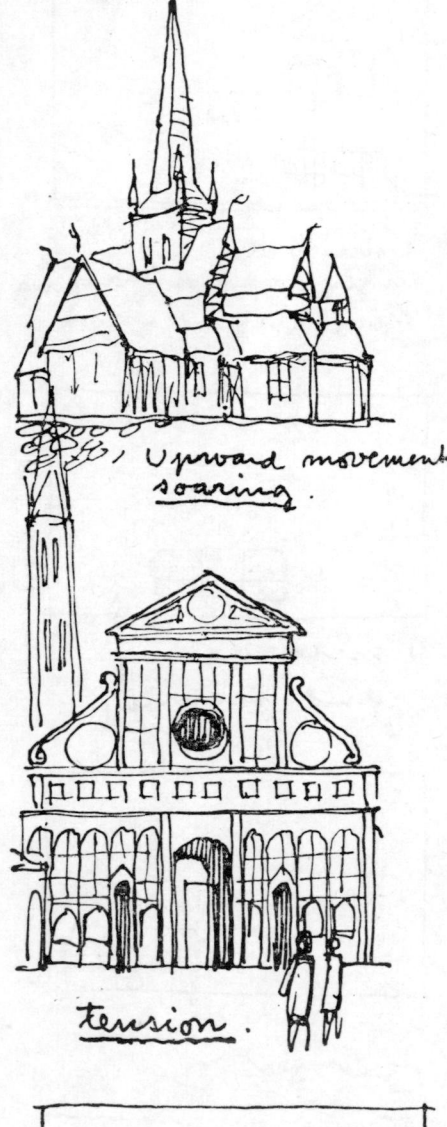

Upward movement, soaring.

tension.

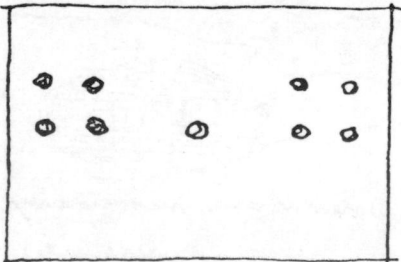

Balance.

18

The church builders of the Middle Ages worked with the opposite effect. They favoured the slender, pointed forms which obviously strove upwards, and in that way they managed to make their buildings seem light, soaring and not of this world. We can like this form of movement as well, for we are the whole time well aware that there is such a thing as gravity and that it will ensure that everything stays in place.

Finally, here is an example of how both effects, the upwards and downwards movements, have been used simultaneously; this is the church gable as the architects of the Renaissance and Baroque liked to build it. Here the pointed gable of the middle part strives upwards, while the spiral ends to the half-gables at the sides go the opposite way. The siting of round windows and other architectural features can further assist in emphasizing this struggle for dominance. Here the desire for a sense of *tension* influences the method and form of construction used.

BALANCE

Now let us go back to our stones again. This time we divide them into two groups of four, laid symmetrically on the table and with the odd stone in the middle. Once again we have a feeling of rest. The whole reminds us of a balance with weights of equal size on either side. Here again it is what we know, this time of the laws of physics, which has a decisive influence on what we see. If we remove the middle point, the picture is not changed, because our eye still labours indefatigably to find system in everything. It has long since drawn a central line right across the table top and on this central line the groups are balanced.

If we can now remember what we know about greater and smaller weights on shorter and larger arms of a lever, we can experiment and see if those laws also coincide with the requirements of the eye. Let us place a solitary stone or two right away from the central line and assemble the others nearer the middle on the other side. And true enough, it still appears to be at rest, in harmony, but this time in a tenser way. The eye has to do a little more work in order to discover that all is as it should be. All the same, the laws of physics cannot be translated absolutely directly into the world of visual impression. This is, amongst other things, because the stones lying by themselves appear larger in bulk to the eye than those which are gathered together. Besides, we do not always have to do, as here, with masses, or bodies; often we are working only with surfaces.

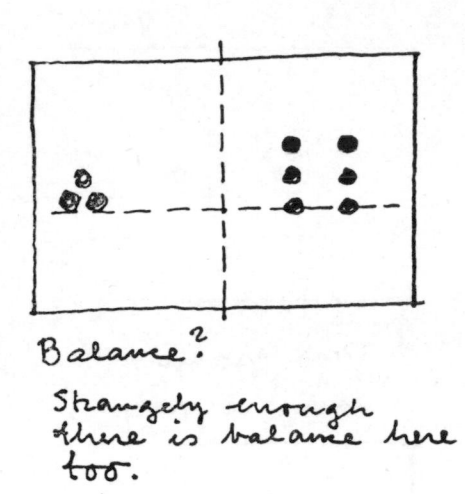

Balance?

Strangely enough there is balance here too.

We can get a white wall and a black window-opening to appear harmonious and balanced, even if we place the window up in one corner. This picture certainly does not agree with the normal illustration of the laws of equilibrium, yet we sense that we are dealing here with related phenomena. The reason for this is that the wall itself has mass and weight. We get that impression even when it is drawn on paper. Its surface is at any rate *something*; it isn't just air.

It is these lessons for which we shall have most practical use: in hanging pictures on a wall, in arranging furniture in a room. If all the furniture is huddled in one corner, it can make us feel as though the whole room was about to tilt over. As a rule it will be the wall's central lines which will be the eye's lines of balance, but there is nothing to prevent us introducing other fulcrums: a large picture, a grandfather clock, or something like that, can be put in as 'axis' round which everything *turns* (to keep to the language of motion).

This tilts.

THE GROUP

We have once or twice used the word *group*, and we ought perhaps to see what that really means. Put two stones on the table, reasonably close to each other, and they will lie there

This balances.

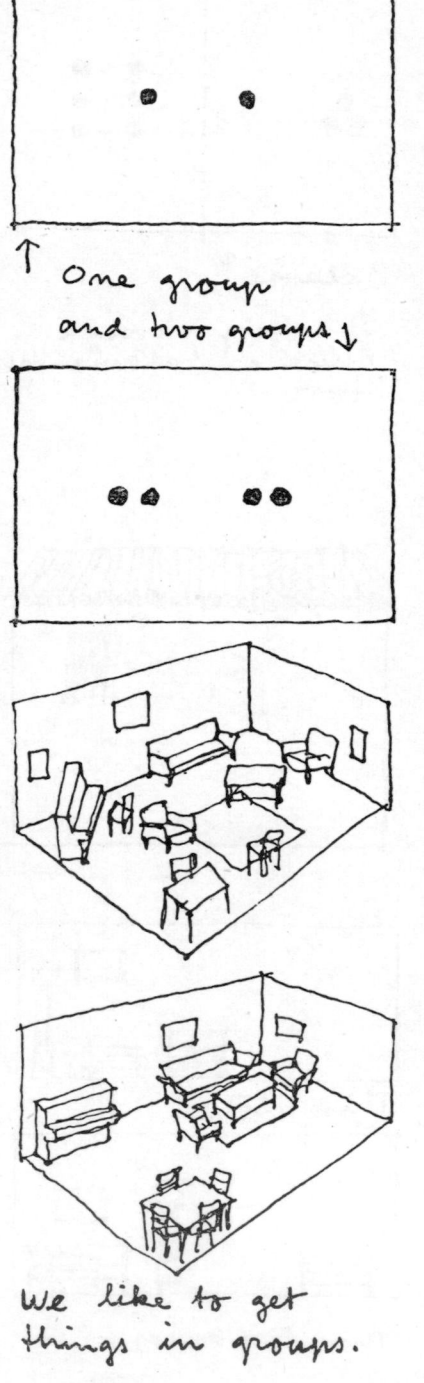

One group
and two groups

We like to get
things in groups.

like two friends who are *together*. If we now take two other stones and put them one on either side of this original group, but with a shorter distance between each and its neighbour than the first two had, then we will see that two new combinations have arisen. The old friends no longer know each other; they have acquired new connections. Here it is our eye which has been at work with its craving to arrange and *unify*. What it sees in the first place is not four stones, but two groups of two. That makes the impression easier to retain as a form.

If, finally, we spread all the stones haphazard all over the table, the total impression is speckly and unrestful, we cannot grasp it. But if we move those lying nearest each other a little closer together, we again get a sort of order. Our attention will be concentrated on what is the predominant unit, then on the next dominant, etc. Here it is the sense of order, of which we spoke earlier, with which we are making closer acquaintance.

In arranging a room practical considerations will help us to work thus with groups, which we will do rather as a matter of course. The dining-table with its chairs forms one area of interest, the rest-group, consisting perhaps of sofa, table and arm-chairs, another. More dominating things like a cupboard or a bureau can afford to stand by themselves, but small objects like a work-table and that kind of thing need something to go with them. The resultant picture is especially sound and good if the groups are so arranged that the eye naturally draws connecting lines between the dominant points in the groups.

LINE

The lines so far mentioned have mostly been invisible ones that we have imagined. But, naturally, lines can also be real and possess the most varied qualities. We shall see that the rules on which the eye works when it has to take in a line's character are closely related to those which govern our actions and our consciousness generally.

We now remove the stones from the table and instead draw a wavy line from one side to the other. When looking at the picture thus made the eye will first and foremost follow this line, in the same way as our entire body would have done had the table-top been a piece of open ground and the line a trodden path.

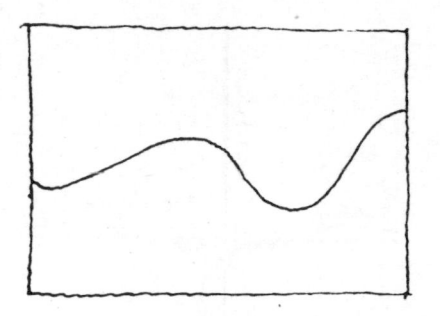

a _soft line_.

If the line describes an unreasonably large curve, like that in the next drawing, our eye will do what we ourselves would have done on open ground, it will take a short cut across the narrow neck at the foot of the bulge. That is, of course, provided there is no obstacle in the way. Expressed as a visual impression: we apprehend this line both as being a continuous stroke and as if it were composed of two elements: a straight line and a ring.

Now, various lines have different effects upon us. There is a certain justification for saying that a straight line seems factual; it is after all the shortest distance between two points, a mathematical and incontrovertible concept. But just as very factual people are seldom particularly amusing, the straight line can be said to seem _dry_ or _severe_. But we cannot dispense with straight lines altogether; they help to keep things in place, to give firm holds for our ideas. A painting can be full of the most restless lines and shapes which would appear quite chaotic if the composition did not have the support of the severe margin of the frame.

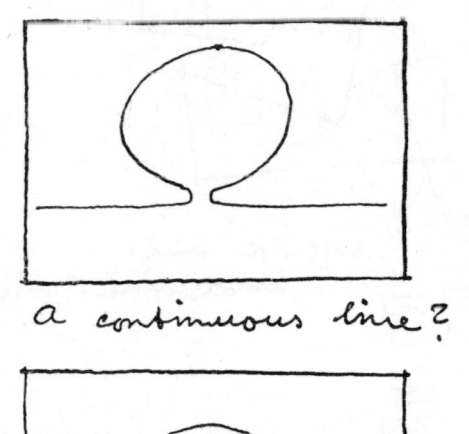

a continuous line?

Or a straight line and a circle?

There are two kinds of straight line which are all but indispensable, the strictly vertical and horizontal. These are the _lines of gravity_, the directions of the plumb on the line and of the surface of still water. They are also those of ourselves when standing erect, seen against the open horizon. They comprise the fixed points of departure for our whole world of form. It is only in amusement parks that

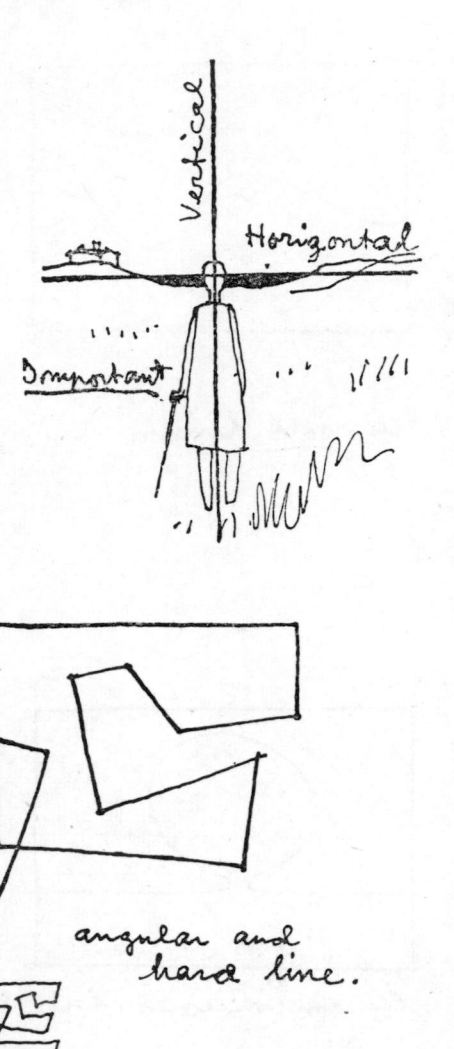

angular and hard line.

But now it isn't angular any longer.

people build houses in which everything is out of the vertical and horizontal, and such houses are so confusing that people are quite bewildered when they come out of them.

A line which has regular curves we associate with something *soft*. The eye follows it with an even movement. But if we draw such a wavy line on the wall of a room, the effect can be nasty and distracting. Unless there are other things to draw our attention away, our eye will be forced to follow its movements up and down till we become quite seasick. This hasn't anything to do with the fact that the line also *reminds* us of sea and waves. A sailor or a farmer from the prairie would have just the same sensation. If such lines are to be used successfully, they must have a definite purpose, lead the eye to some place or other where it can find repose after its wandering.

A line which makes abrupt and violent bends, like that drawn here, we would most certainly call *restless*. It is like having to walk along a street which keeps taking unexpected bends, we become confused, grow tired of having to turn sharp corners, and we easily lose our sense of direction. Our eye would feel aggrieved if it had to go on many such expeditions. Is it not curious, though, how lines which do not 'represent' anything can yet speak to us in this way, tell us so much? But so it is, and the more we know about these things, the more plainly will they speak to us.

If we now take this piece of restless line and reduce it in size considerably and at the same time turn it into a sort of chain by adding several links of the same kind, we will get an entirely different situation. It no longer seems restless, because the eye is no longer able to follow it along all its squiggles and bends. The eye closes it up, takes short cuts and gets just the one impression of it as an entity. It is as though it had become a straight line again, only having acquired a kind of thickness. This thickness contains something which we can call a *pattern*, and the pattern is

22

repeated, so that we get the feeling that the line consists of several links. We have simplified it and grouped it, and we have every right to say that this thick line is also richer, or more amusing, than a black line of corresponding thickness.

Much of what we have learned here can be applied to our surroundings without further explanation. But some of it must wait till we can see it in its wider connections.

VOLUME AND MASS

So far we have regarded the stones used in our experiments really just as dots or spots on a surface. Let us now pick one up and examine it: weigh it in one hand and inspect it from every angle. We then see that it has weight and girth. But it does not have any marked *shape*: we know it as a stone, but it is difficult to describe it more precisely.

If we now chip bits off it until we have turned it into a cube, the situation immediately becomes quite different. We have then *formed* something, made a shape which we can not only describe and reproduce more or less accurately, but which is in its very being bound by the laws of geometry. We can, for example, say that its superficies is made up of six equal quadrilateral surfaces, and thereby its entire character is completely described. It cannot be anything but a cube, however we turn and twist it. The smoother and more even we can make the surfaces, the sharper will the edges and corners become, and the more exact will its shape appear.

What sort of impression does this cube make on us? Is it ugly or beautiful, or just nothing at all? It doesn't perhaps arouse our enthusiasm, but all the same we will call it beautiful because it has the appearance of something absolute, something of eternal validity. Any fresh interference with its shape would mean that its quality of cube

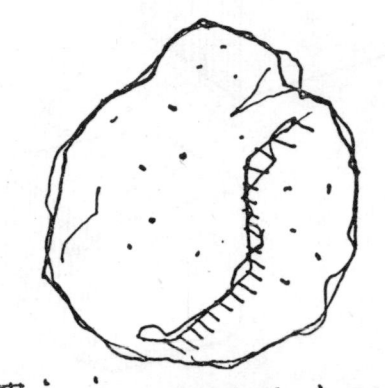

This is supposed to be a (shapeless) stone.

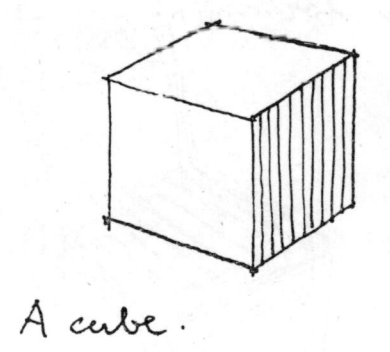

A cube.

Above, an exact cube. Below, the same with rounded edges. It now appears to be heavier.

This empire chair is precise, i.e. light in form.

would at once be destroyed. Again it is our *knowledge* of the fact that its structure is in accordance with the physical laws which causes us to apprehend it as a *form*, and an immensely clear and fixed form at that.

There is, though, one thing we can do to it without it altogether losing its *character* of cube. Let us do this and see if that will make its nature and characteristics plainer to us. What we do is slightly round off all its corners and edges. That makes it, of course, somewhat smaller, but the effect is to make it *appear* astonishingly much smaller. That is so, at any rate, as long as we don't look at it from straight in front, for it still measures the same across. It seems as though the cube's superficies had somehow drawn closer round it, had shrunk on to it, without the mass being altered to any noticeable extent. If this really were the case, then the cube would have become more compact and its specific gravity would have become greater. And that is exactly what the effect is. We can also express it by saying that the new cube appears *heavier*.

This experiment brings to our attention a new characteristic of the original, pure cube. We assumed that it was cut from a stone, that it was solid, but we can't *see* that. Someone who had not seen it fashioned could just as well imagine that it was made of thin plates and was hollow. But when the edges are rounded off that impression vanishes. It is still possible that there might be a space inside, but we imagine that the walls must at least be thick enough to permit the rounding-off of their edges. On this basis, too, the second cube appears heavier than the first.

If we want our furniture to appear light and airy, we naturally start by making the dimensions of all legs, thick surfaces and such as slender and thin as possible. But this effect can be enhanced by making the forms exact, by making surfaces really flat and corners sharp. The Empire or Regency style, which developed at the beginning of the

24

nineteenth century, used just those effects. The chair shown on page 24 is from that period. The lines are simple and precise, the legs have a sharp, square section, and all other edges are also made sharp. It appears to be austere and light. If we put this another way, using words which better describe what the makers of the chair were trying to express by those means, we can say that the whole thing has the character of *distinguished elegance*. Polished manners and assured demeanour, in contrast to the robust, merry or greedy.

A house with markedly level wall surfaces, as they can be when we build in concrete, will also give the impression of being light. This effect can be emphasized by putting the windows flush with the face of the wall so that its thickness cannot be seen. When that is done we will unquestioningly imagine it as quite thin. This sense of lightness thus has nothing to do with the actual weight of the material used in the construction. But if you ask what other kinds of sensation these qualities release, it is not easy to give a plain answer. Other effects also have a part to play and determine the final result. But let us stick to the quality of elegance, which can be both good and bad. To a certain extent it is right to associate lightness with civilized living: all unnecessary things have been pared away and we have learned to make the construction in a rational way, that is, with the minimum of material. We can also say that what is light gives the impression of being friendly and accommodating, at any rate it symbolizes the opposite of the portcullis. But if this lightness is exaggerated the effect can be of something rickety and flimsy. We in Norway say of houses which are too 'light' that they seem *cold*, because, with our climate, we are inclined to equate solidity and warmth.

A log cabin with a turf roof and all sharpness taken from its corners by the intersecting logs, is a *heavy* house, at least

light house of concrete (clear surfaces and corners) —

— and heavy house of wood (coarse surfaces, indistinct corners).

House of 1915. Its heavy form is stressed by the way it is drawn.

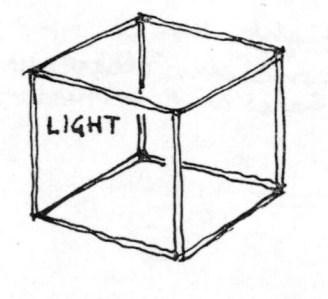

LIGHT

The Japanese house looks very light

that is the impression it gives. This heaviness gives us a sense of snugness and security, but it can also give an impression of grimness if it is over-emphasized. We are then made to think of prisons and fortifications. In the first decades of the twentieth century architects were fond of heavy house forms, which they produced preferably by using broken roof surfaces, bays and other things which veiled the main shape. We can regard this tendency as the expression of a feeling for good craftsmanship combined with a delight in good solid materials like hand-made bricks and good stout beams. In many ways it was a reaction to the inferior, cheaper materials which industry was producing, and this latter is a point to which we must return later.

We can make another kind of cube, not of stone this time, but of twelve thin pieces of wire of equal length, which we solder together at the corners. It is debatable whether this really is a cube—at any rate our first definition no longer seems to fit, since, strictly speaking, it is not composed of surfaces. But here our eye is again working away on its own; it imagines these surfaces with which it fills in the firm outlines. It is impossible to imagine an effect of greater lightness than is given by this. Anything to do with mass has been removed, and the whole thing is rather the representation of a cube, than a cube itself. It can be as light as thought.

In terms of houses, we will get these same effects when the walls are pierced with large light-apertures. This is especially true when the windows are placed in or near the corners, so that the light can shine right through. A structure that in itself is massive will give a similar impression of being airy, if it is surrounded by open verandas with a roof on thin pillars; and in such cases we can safely translate the idea of lightness as a friendly and welcoming attitude. Disengaged pillars have always been a popular element in architecture. Not only do they afford a wealth of possibilities for the interplay of light and shade, but they give the eye something to work on in the shape of imaginary planes and surfaces which airily fill in the whole composition.

The *sphere* is as much bound by laws as the cube, and just as basic. A sphere is a sphere, whether it is large or small, red or blue, whether it is made of stone or of wood. For reasons which we have already mentioned, it gives the impression of being naturally exceedingly dense and massive. And we know, too, from geometry that a space, a volume, cannot be enclosed more economically than by the surface of a sphere. That is why it appears so firm and fine.

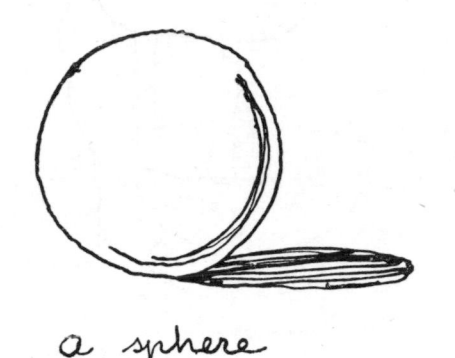

a sphere

If we now place the sphere and the first cube side by side, we soon discover fresh characteristics in them both. The cube suddenly seems angular and *hard*, while the sphere gives the impression of something soft, quite irrespective of the material of which it may be made. It is easy to see why this is. We think the cube hard, because we cannot help thinking what it would be like to bump ourselves on its sharp corners and edges. Even if we hang it up under the ceiling, we will still be unable to avoid the thought. The sphere, on the other hand, has none of those dangers. But these forms suggest other notions as well.

We think that the cube must necessarily be made of something pretty hard to be able to keep its shape, for it to be possible to make those flat surfaces and straight edges. But the sphere could easily have been made from a lump of soft clay. It would be senseless to try and discover whether the one is more beautiful than the other because of this; each is equally good in its own way. But if they are to be *used* for something, whether for a utilitarian purpose, or in the composition of a picture, then these special qualities at once come to the fore and we judge each differently.

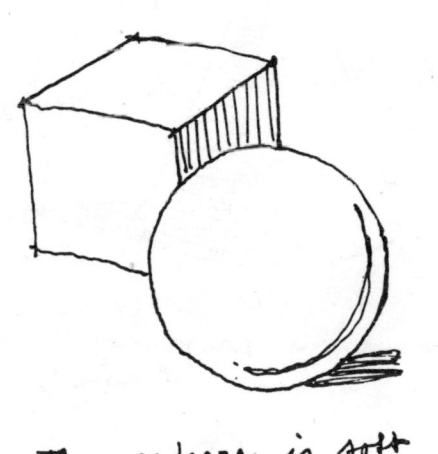

The sphere is <u>soft</u> and <u>firm</u>.
The cube <u>hard</u> and <u>angular</u>.

In daily life we find the soft round spherical shape in just those places where protection is needed, as casing and coverings for all sorts of modern mechanical equipment.

27

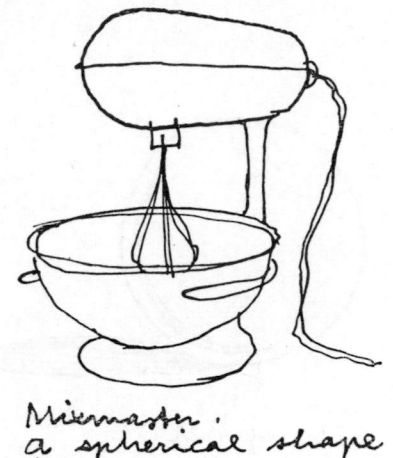

Mixmaster.
a spherical shape
is good both for
cleanliness and
perfection.

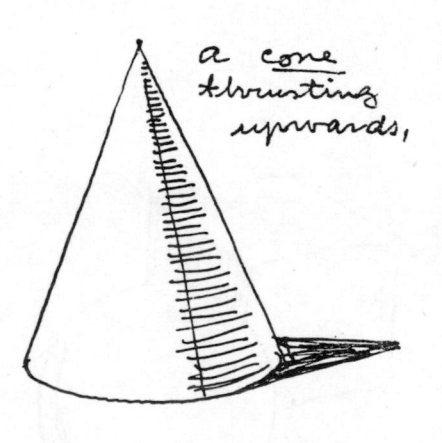

a cone
thrusting
upwards,

and one pressing
down.

Otherwise we meet the sphere almost only as decoration on things which have a certain amount of ornamentation.

We now introduce a further shape into our experimental team, a tall, pointed cone. Let us see what that has to tell us. While the cube and the sphere gave us the impression of being altogether at rest, unchangeable and always the same however we twisted and turned them, the cone is a restless figure. Its character changes according to whether it is lying down or standing up, and it never seems to be satisfied with the situation. It appears to be in motion, in the same way as we found with the stones on the table-top. If we set it with its point upwards, it gives the impression of soaring. But the cone is not a definite geometrical concept in the same sense as the cube or the sphere. Its height can be varied in relation to the diameter of its base.

If we make it low, we will get movement in the opposite direction, for it then seems as though the cone was collapsing and spreading out over the table. But somewhere or other there must be a height at which even this unhappy soul will come to rest. We can try drawing different triangles on a piece of paper and see if we can discover where this height lies.

We now arrange the cube, the tall cone and the sphere one alongside the other, and we see that we have made a little story, a chain of events. First we experience the calm, somewhat severe and steadfast cube, and as soon as we have clearly grasped its shape, we are swept off upwards by the cone. Then, when we can go no further, we make our way back, and our gaze falls to rest on the ultimate enfolding form of the sphere. It is like a little drama, perhaps not so very exciting, but made up of appropriate effects. It is those effects artists use in the composition of their paintings and sculptures. The architect does the same, and even when he is working with simple architectural bodies, the mere grouping of them can be done with great and dramatic effect, if they are consciously put together. The same is true of the grouping of things in a room, even though here the effects will be less marked. That, however, brings us back to the room. The concept of room, or space, is itself one which calls for analysis.

SPACE

We now leave the simple, more or less law-bound figures and introduce a fresh one of more complicated character, as the drawing shows. If we were to describe it briefly we would perhaps say that it was a cube with a semi-cylindrical groove cut out of it. We thus immediately assume that something has been taken away, no matter how the groove was actually arrived at. The result has been to form a cavity, or quite simply, a space inside the figure.

The extraordinary thing about this space is that it seems to continue even outside the actual area of the figure. Having established that the inside cavity seems to be formed of the half lateral section of a cylinder, we can also fix the limits of its imaginary continuation: that is, the other half of the cylinder, the first half of which fits into the cavity. The eye is indefatigable, and here it at once completes the picture at which the figure in a way hints.

That is why a semicircular niche in a wall has a certain attraction. Even when we are outside the niche we will have the feeling of being within its sphere of interest, its space, as long as we are within the invisible circle comprised by the continuation of the niche's floor area. A bow window can have the same effect. It is an opening outwards which has a simultaneous effect inwards into the room, dividing it up and making it more exciting.

In the late seventeenth and early eighteenth centuries architects were very keen on these phenomena, especially

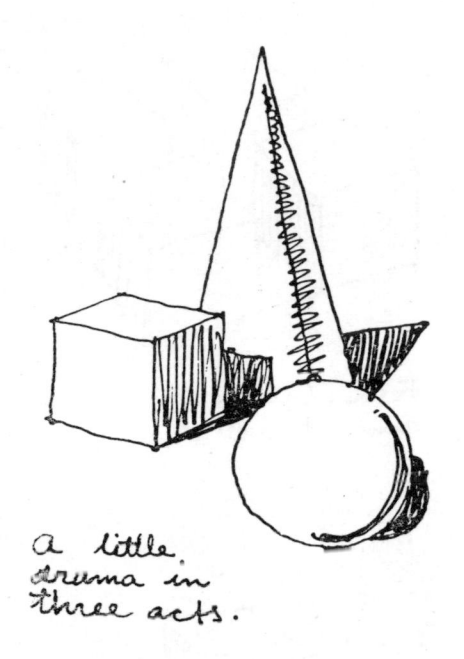

a little drama in three acts.

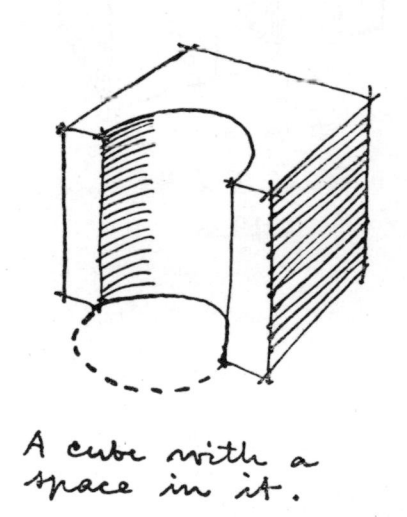

A cube with a space in it.

29

Four bricks
and that's all.

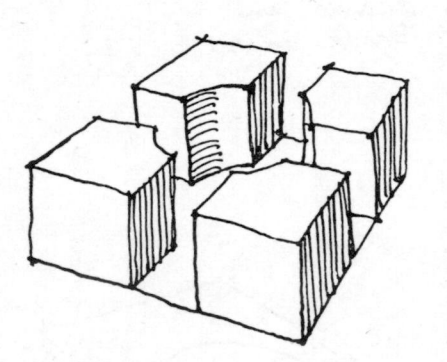

Four bricks and
a space.

for the external façades of buildings giving on to streets or squares. A straight street, lined by straight walls on either side, must almost be considered a nullity, a fortuitous fissure, a distance between the houses on either side.

Now, put niches in the walls and at once it is as though you had created considerable space in the picture of the street, whether this is actually so or not. It is no longer just the houses which are the picture; now the street itself is in it; gives its own effect of space. It is especially obvious if we imagine the intersection of two streets. If the four houses at the corners have square corners, we get an indeterminate crossing devoid of character. But if we imagine the corners shorn off there will at once be a certain effect of room, a 'space' between the houses. This effect will be even greater if we make the shorn-off bits concave, so that their base-lines form part of a circle which has the middle of the space as its centre. That gives the eye a definite course to follow, and it will itself draw a line, that is the circumference, all the way round.

It can be asked why architects have not used these effects in all ages. The answer is that in the eighteenth century people began to work with the picture of a town as a whole to a much larger extent than had been done before. Architects had a much better grasp of what they were about, could plan larger and more complex units, and for this they had the guidance of comprehensive laws and directions as to how they were to be built. Before that, it had been deemed sufficient to mark out the line of streets, leaving the final form of the buildings in them more or less to the individual builder. Integrated planning in all spheres of life was a development of the eighteenth century when they took a delight in giving full play to it in the spacing of their towns.

Interest in space can be regarded as the opposite of interest in the *thing*. The Greeks had worked with large integrating plans for their cities, and especially for their great temples like those we can see at Delphi, the Parthenon at Athens, and elsewhere. Here, however, there is no trace of any endeavour to bring out the space-forming elements. The actual spaces, the temple interiors themselves, seem to have been of subordinate significance. This is because the Greeks were exclusively occupied by the details and by the compact, self-sufficient and perfectly valid form of the individual buildings. You might not violate any of that just in order to attain other effects. Probably we would be right to equate tendencies of this kind and an individualistic attitude to life.

Modern architecture is again occupied with the problem of space, though in a new way. To us it seems senseless to treat individual buildings as though they were just masses; compact lumps which you can carve into as you think fit. We feel that this is to do violence to everything which is to take place inside, so that the aim of our plan can no longer develop freely and harmoniously. Such functional considerations plus those of economy have led to the exteriors of our buildings often being most simple and un-complicated. This, however, makes it all the more important that the interplay of the various structures should be rich and exciting, something which can be achieved pre-eminently by working with space effects in streets, squares and integrated lay-outs. It is not essential to use cylindrical planes or arcs of circles, even though such elements often give the most distinct picture, which is why they have been used as examples here.

In the cube we made of steel wires, we also formed a space, a cubic space bounded by the twelve side-lines. The feature of this cube, which distinguished it from all the others we have studied, is that what chiefly attracts our attention is not its external form, but what is inside it, the space made there. This space is not enclosed in any way, there is no direct division between the air there and that

St. Carlo Quattro
Fontane, Rome.
Baroque.
Curving walls provide
a number of different
space effects in the
street picture.

31

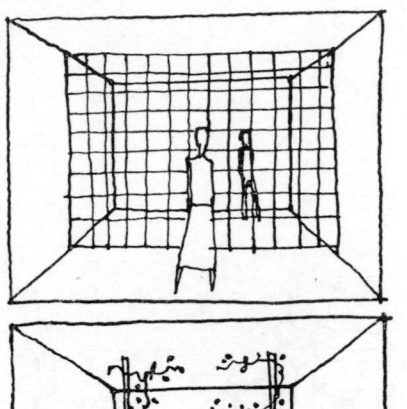

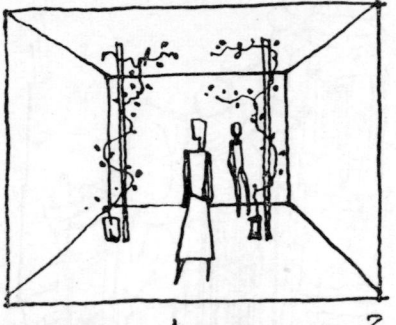

One or two rooms?

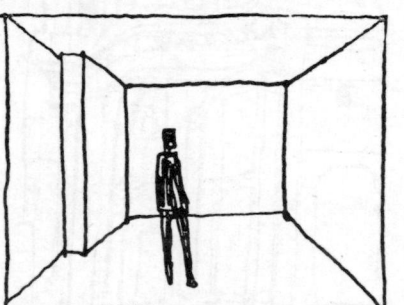

an irregular room

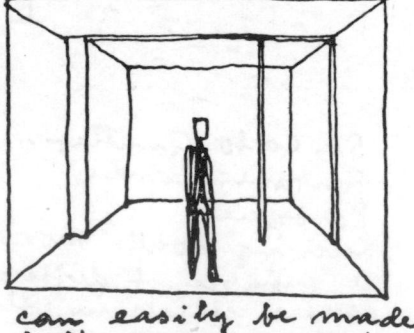

can easily be made
both more compact
and richer.

outside; in fact, it is debatable whether in such a case we can talk about 'outside' and 'inside' at all. None the less, we are in no doubt that our space has its distinct limits. This brings us to something very remarkable and most important for the actual furnishing and arrangement of rooms.

If we divide a room laterally with a perpendicular wall of netting, we will get a very definite impression that it is really divided into two. Yet at the same time the effect is quite different from what it would have been if the division had been made by an ordinary wall. With the netting the whole impression is *richer*, if we can put it that way. We have the feeling of there being two rooms, yet at the same time we can see them both as one; it is as though we were having two experiences, seeing two pictures at the same time.

Not many people would want to use such a net-wall, but it is possible to simplify the idea by erecting two slender poles from floor to ceiling and, if we feel we need an excuse for them, we can say that they are to act as supports for creepers or other indoor plants with which we wish to decorate our room. This will still give the impression of a distinct division and greater richness in the effect of the space. It gives us a *foreground* and a *background*, and those together tend to give the room greater depth. We can also use such effects to differentiate between the different parts of a room according to the uses to which it is put: a dining compartment and a sitting-room part, or whatever it may be.

If the room's shape is cut up, like that in the drawing in the margin, it can be difficult to get any effect of space. It is to a certain extent formless, difficult for the eye to grasp. If we introduce our flower poles or other space-forming factors at the right place, we will get the room divided into two distinct main shapes, each easy to command, simple and good to the eye, at the same time as the total experience is retained.

CLOSED FORM

Here are some examples of how light elements like pegs and cross-pieces can influence our conception of the main form. Let us draw any ordinary small chair, as light and simple in construction as it can be made. Here we conceive of the four legs as more or less independent elements, and the result is that the main form seems rather indeterminate, restless and straddled. Usually this does not matter very much, for in real life the legs don't end in the air, as here, but stand firmly on a solid floor, which has an integrating effect on the total picture.

Chair with "open" form.

Now let us take a typical sixteenth-century chair. It has perpendicular legs which are joined low down, almost at the level of the floor, by four cross-pieces. This makes the chair more solid, and the people of those days also liked to have bars to put their feet on, so as to get them out of the cold draught on the floors. But in all probability along with this utilitarian purpose went a desire to do something with the form of the chair, which thereby has received a decisive addition to its character: from consisting of separate legs the underpart of the chair has become an integrated unit, a cube or what approximates to the form of a cube. In the sixteenth century, people were busy giving expression to man's ability for precise thought, for sticking to mathematical and geometrical concepts. They liked to think that everything was solid and well ordered, and they fashioned their dwellings along those lines.

Chair with closed form. Renaissance.

There is no need yet to form an opinion about such tendencies, and it will be enough here to notice the interesting fact that four cross-pieces can make an object, in this case a chair, change its entire character, depending on whether we place them higher up or lower down.

In the margin below we have a sort of house with three rooms, no roof, and also no doors or windows. There is no doubt that the effect is of an enclosed, shut-in space, so shut in that we would become quite distracted if we were put into it.

We must remember that the house, with its enclosed space, is a sort of emergency contrivance for us humans. It gives us protection, snugness and warmth, and in modern life it is those or cognate feelings which dominate our experience of space. But in the depths of our beings we still have a horror of being shut in, of being lured into a prison, a trap. We look round for ways of escape, and that is why we at once have a slight feeling of uneasiness if the windows are placed a little too high up the walls. In markedly enclosed spaces, like cinemas or broadcasting studios, this uneasiness can become quite noticeable—and with many people it is a definite form of nervous suffering, called *claustrophobia*.

Conversely, the feeling of being entirely unprotected can also induce fear, the fear which makes most people prefer to have their bed up against a wall rather than standing by itself in the middle of the floor. It is good to have your back covered. At sea or on the great plains it is possible for people to feel oppressed. This sensation is known as *agoraphobia*, fear of open places. But let us get back to our examples.

In the drawing on the following page, windows have been inserted in all the external walls and the rooms themselves made to communicate with each other and the outside world by doors set in line.

Thus, openings have now been made, yet they have been so placed that they have little effect on the shut-in, solid character of the rooms. In essentials the rooms have scarcely been changed at all. If we are to have any experience of the

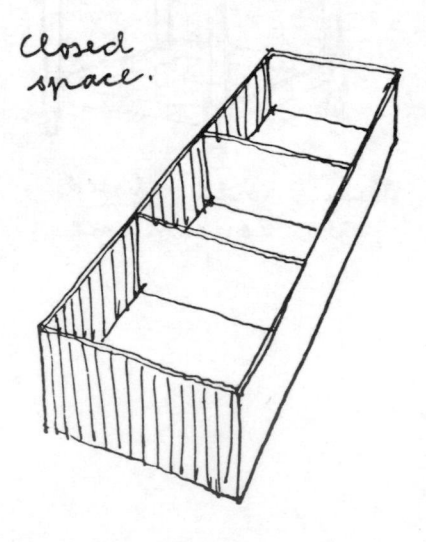

Closed space.

three rooms as one (assuming that we are restricted to moving about the floors) we shall have to stand somewhere on the axis which can be drawn through the doors. The picture we will thus get is quite definite, and there it is drawn in the margin.

You will observe that we don't see much of the individual rooms, but, on the other hand, the passage between them appears long and *impressive*, because the impression of length is increased by the foreshortening of perspective which becomes progressively greater with every room inwards. These effects were continually used in seventeenth- and eighteenth-century building. You can say that the architects of those periods worked with perspective as a 'lawful' means in architecture—built their compositions on it. The use of this principle also meant, however, that you only got the full, or intended, enjoyment from the building if you stood at a certain point or moved along a definite line. Thus we are perhaps right in regarding these architectural forms as correspondingly severe. They give the beholder orders, lay down how things are to be taken in a thoroughly unilateral way. At any rate, there is no doubt that the very societies, the same people who hit upon the idea of working with these effects, were also ordered in equally strict social systems, which eventually led to the absolute monarchies. Then, of course, the lengthy, severe axis-effects were excellently suited for deferential approach, and the king himself could be even more impressive seated on a throne at the end of the inmost room of all. All the lines ran together round his person.

No one can deny the effects of perspective, but instead of taking them into account as things which exist, they can also be included among the optical *illusions*, things which confuse our notions of the real size of things. Two men at different distances will seem to be different in height, when in reality they are equally tall. Modern architecture prefers

Here doors have been made along a central axis.
To a visitor a would appear like this ↓

to work with forms which are not based on this use of perspective.

In the margin is a drawing of a sort of house with three rooms. We have used the same solid walls as before, but shifted them so that now there are openings along the sides. Here there is no possibility of viewing all the rooms as one, but on the other hand we have the feeling that the one room is shoving itself into the next, and this movement is continued, so that there is a feeling of connection all the way. And we have this feeling wherever we stand. But to get an impression of the whole we have to move about. The act of experience thus forces the observer to a certain activity, but in that he also obtains the possibility of getting more out of the whole.

Such a treatment of space is thus not authoritarian. All are equal there. There is no central place. We will notice, too, that the areas round the house are not 'outside' to the same degree as before, for there, too, space is formed which is linked with the rooms inside, so that it is difficult to say where the one begins and the other ends.

It is reasonable that room-forms of this kind have been accorded a certain place in modern architecture, where for reasons of economy you are often forced to work with small dimensions, though you don't want to lose the sense of spaciousness and possibility for movement. In this way, too, there is greater *tension*, a thing we can very well do with when we have renounced a number of architectural decorative effects. Perhaps, too, its sauntering freedom is more in keeping with the spirit of the times.

RHYTHM

The thumping heart, the pulse beating under one's skin, are symbols of life itself, mysterious and strangely attractive. All regular repetition has the same effect: waves

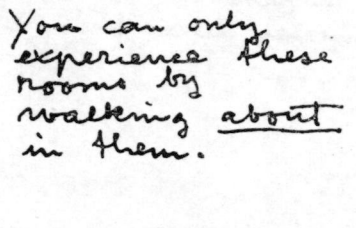

You can only experience these rooms by walking about in them.

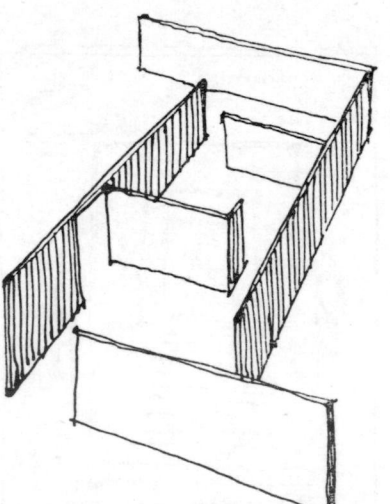

36

rolling up a beach, branches waving in the wind, the shiny pendulum behind the little window in the clock-case. There can be the same mystery in sound, and the drum is probably the oldest of all instruments.

The actual significance of the various form-rhythms is probably as difficult to explain as it is to say why the waltz and the samba affect us in such entirely different ways. Yet this comparison itself tells us quite a lot, for the phenomena are closely related.

We get the simplest of all form-rhythms if we place similar figures at equal intervals one from another, e.g., as windows in a façade. This is a completely even rhythm, like when we hear someone walking steadily along a street. Just as boring, you might also say, if you are one of those who hold that everything ought to be amusing, whatever else it isn't.

If we put the windows together in pairs, we get a more exciting rhythm, in that more seems to be happening. It is no longer an even pacing, but rather a jumping effect. But we can also arrange the windows in threes and at the same time make some variation in their relative height (which we would obviously take care not to do if they were real windows in a house). That really puts life into the rhythm, for we have introduced movement. Just like a hare's track in the snow, they remind us of hop, skip and a jump. Obviously there is something jolly going on.

These examples were very schematic. The notion of rhythm can be introduced into all sorts of constellations of forms, as repetition of lines, of surfaces, as recurrence of certain proportions. To a certain extent we can say that the demand for units of equal size, already discussed, is itself a demand for rhythm, but by using the actual word 'rhythm' we do require something more; that is, that there should also be within those units something which links them together, makes us see them as a sequence. And it is

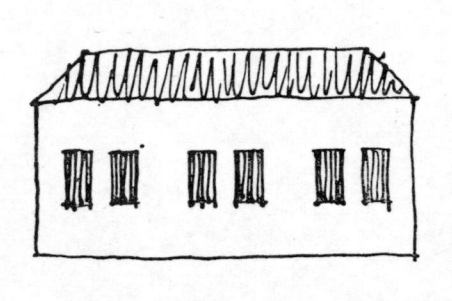

Even, –

more restless,

and jerky rhythms.

this sequence which is the secret and power of rhythm; it is as though you must also have the help of *time* in order to comprehend it all properly. You feel debarred from registering the whole object you are looking at in one glance, your eye has to follow the elements of the rhythm step by step. And this, perhaps wholly imaginary process, makes the entire experience richer because it has involved a considerable effort.

We took the house and windows as our point of departure, but it must be emphasized that usually it is the lesser things, ornamentation and pattern, in which rhythm is made to appear, at any rate in its simplest sense. Here most people will consider the requirement of rhythmical repetition something almost in the nature of a law. Or, to put it the other way round, the pattern and ornamentation will have been put there to allow such a rhythmical play to be introduced. But we can also speak of a rhythmical construction of a chair. By that we will mean that there are certain proportions which recur, or it can be a question of the rhythmical building up of different planes. But we must remember that these proportions and planes do not all need to be real—many can just be indicated by the expedients we described previously.

It is difficult to delve any deeper into these matters in a general description. You have to train your eye, make your way along by a process of experiment. Nor is this the place to attempt an explanation of *why* the whole thing can seem so fascinating. Some things can be left to be themselves, to tell their own story.

NOW WE KNOW SOMETHING ABOUT FORM

We have now gone through some simple but decisive rules for what is meant by form, and we have also tried to find out what is the immediate effect upon us of some of these forms. That, however, is by no means the end of our analysis.

The forms we have so far discussed have all been of a very definite kind. They are forms which we have been able to register because of the eye's direct agency. Or they have had a connection with something we know from mathematics or geometry. On the other hand, they have no connection with our experiences of the usefulness of things: what purpose they serve, what they are made for, how they are made and other material considerations. Such a method of considering things we call *abstract*. The word really means 'regarded on their own', which in this case means that we have disregarded all the points just mentioned, and confined ourselves to what had to do with the immediate visual impression. When in daily talk we speak of abstract form, we often mean forms which do not 'represent' anything or which have no definite background of experience or use. An 'abstract' painting is a picture which tries to give us a certain experience, to impart a certain mood, through the interplay of planes and forms and without the use of factors which actuate our recollection of other experiences. A form-giver must always be familiar with the abstract means and keep them before his mind's eye. The impression a chair gives us is dependent on our experience of its use, but however good it is to sit on, that does not mean that it is beautiful. Form and line lead their own independent lives on the abstract plane.

The more we *know*, the better acquainted we are with the lawfulness and inner cohesion of the world of abstract form, the more forms we will be able to comprehend, grasp and experience. Our thought will fill them with a certain content.

In the margin is a drawing of a Grecian vase from the fifth century B.C. Some scientist discovered that its curve is shaped with mathematical exactitude as a hyperbola,

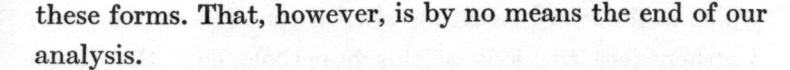

Grecian vase, based on the hyperbola.

which is the curve resulting when a cone is cut obliquely. Further, that the axis of this hyperbola cuts the vase's central axis together with the horizontal plane which can be drawn through the eyelets in the spiral-shaped decorations. It is to be noted too that the Greeks at that time were already to a certain extent familiar with the hyperbola as a mathematical phenomenon. This is not to say that the man who made this vase was an expert mathematician or that he was aware of all this. Yet one way or another these forms must have been emphasized, have found their way into the general consciousness and become important. Nor is it mere chance that the vase is Grecian, for the Greeks had a passion for precision, for what could only be done in one way and not otherwise. This is a further example of the connection between new understanding and new form.

However, there is also room in the picture for the other way in which we apprehend things, that which is linked to our experience of material things. And that introduces an entirely different form of knowledge about the essence of things, the concept which we call *character* and which is particularly associated with examples in *Nature*.

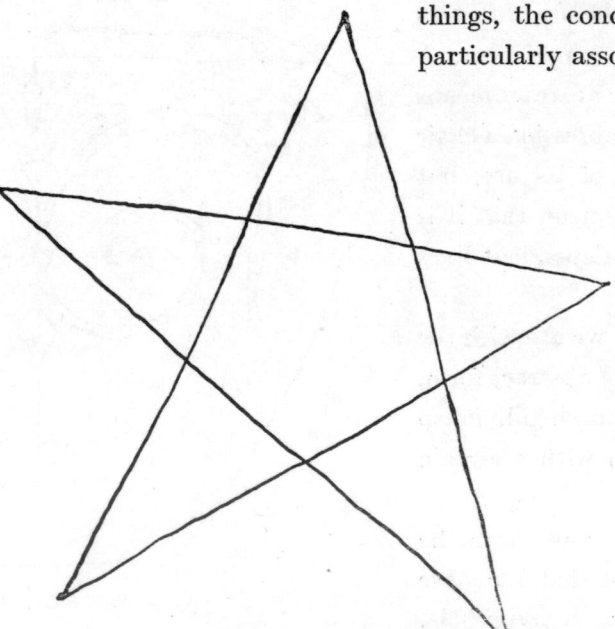

CHAPTER THREE

Which deals with the form-language of Nature and with the concept called character.

We are often told that we are living in the age of technique and in our homes we will find much evidence that this is so. We are surrounded by a number of technical things from electric irons to complicated radio and television sets. They, of course, have helped to influence our opinion of the nature of things. If we have been living in a big city for a long time, it is easy to imagine the whole world as a place of nothing but streets and houses, factories, cars, buses and railway lines, and that all the people wear the same sort of clothes as they go to the same sort of offices or businesses, where all the things they work with are made by human hands and what they do just helps to make everything we do, think and handle more and more distinctly man-made.

But if we go on a flight in an aeroplane we will soon have it forced upon us that all that we have made, all our houses and towns, roads and railways, only amount to a few tiny specks and strips in the landscape. All the rest is *Nature*. In some places, Nature has come in contact with the hand of man, as in fields and pastures, but even these are minute compared with the interminable areas of mountains, forests, steppes and water which lie quite untouched by anything man has done. In the direct sense, of course, we have forced Nature out of our rooms, but we remain aware that it still surrounds us on all sides, in spite of everything,

Fine construction of the fir cone.

and we do everything we can to retain contact with it. In most people's opinion no house can be a *home* until there are flowers in it.

The world of the technicians is quite new. If we measure its age in decades, we can almost count them on our fingers. And taking the long view, so, too, is the whole period which we call that of our *civilization*, which is characterized by man having surrounded himself with things he has himself made. We reckon that we have existed on earth for somewhere around 600,000 years, and of these it is only the last 17,000 which are covered by the period during which we have been conscious of ourselves and our peculiarity, and have developed our ability to think consecutively about things.

In the previous chapter we spoke of cubes and spheres as definite invariable concepts. But it is obvious that these forms, however much we regard them as of eternal validity, are 'inventions', or discoveries, at which we arrived at a relatively late stage in our history, and which each individual has to *learn* for himself. It is different with Nature. Its essence and its forms have become woven into our consciousness in the course of thousands of years; they live in us as instincts.

We can enjoy the beauty in a geometrical figure, or in some perfect article of use, but there is no deeper experience of externals than that associated with Nature's own productions. They, after all, depict the miracle itself, that which is so mysteriously created by the universal forces and by that unfathomable thing we call *life*. As children we have all played with shells and fir-cones, queer stones and glossy chestnuts which we have kept in our pockets, branches we have cut to make bows and arrows, or just to have in our hands, flowers and leaves we have picked; all these things form the actual foundation for a sense of the nature of things, for a knowledge of stuff and materials, an understanding of what is beautiful. Even people who have never been outside the streets of some big city will have the same feelings, because in the last resort they are themselves products of the same natural forces.

Nature has also provided all the materials which through the ages we have used to make our houses and furniture, chiefly clay, stone and wood. The same goes for the clothes we have put on to protect ourselves against the cold and wet, or to deck ourselves: animal skins, wool from sheep, silk from caterpillars, flax and cotton from plants in the ground. Metals have helped us, making the things easier to obtain and enabling us to manufacture them better. All these things we have been able to use in a more or less pure or unadulterated state. For a long time there were very few products which were synthetic; that is to say, composed of natural products combined in such a way as to give a result which appeared to be a new stuff altogether. Glass was one of these. It is only in our day that the artificial stuffs, which are so made and treated that we can no longer see at once what they are made of, have become general. There are all the different plastic materials and pulps, and also such things as ferro-concrete and other building materials. But these products, which are a great help and a joy to us, have also had a confusing effect on our feeling for form and have made it necessary for us to look at certain things rather differently. We think that these materials are in a way difficult to deal with, for they do not speak to us so directly.

This new situation has made us realize that we need an anchor in Nature, which despite all the changes of the times will give us a permanent and unalterable point of fixture. The situation is not new—we have only to think of Jean-Jacques Rousseau, who called upon his age to go "back to Nature", as he thought mankind had gone too far in trusting to its intelligence and ability to think.

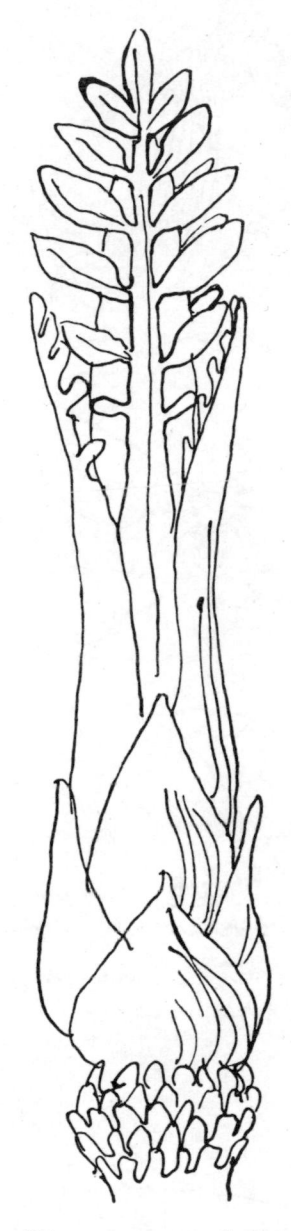

The sprouting plant fills us with wonder.

43

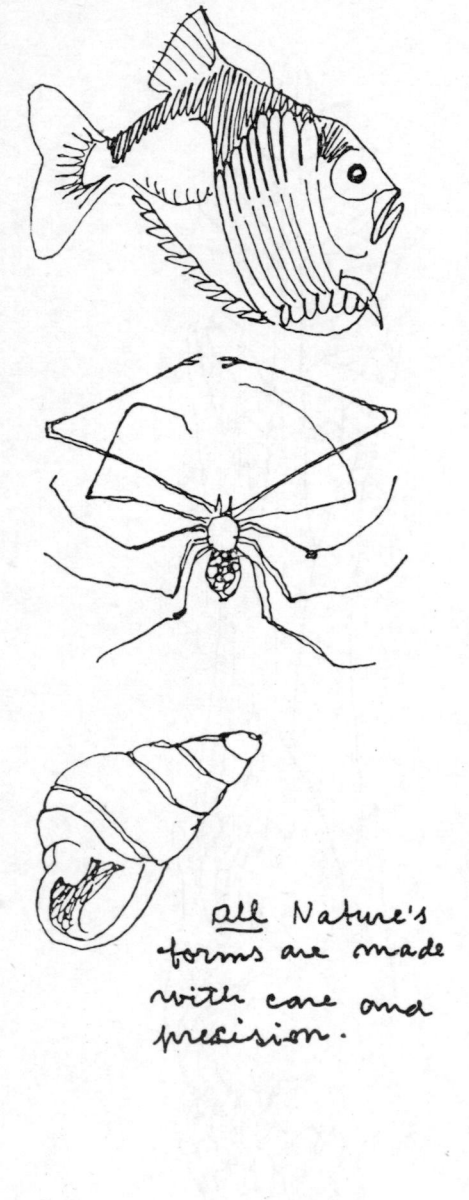

Everything in Nature is beautiful. That, of course, is just an assertion and it won't be easy to prove it. But it is a thing we can say, because we are *agreed* about it; it is accepted, in the same way as in mathematics we are agreed that $a + a = 2a$. We call a product of Nature, for example a maple tree, beautiful because it appears to us to be perfect of its kind. And we call it perfect because we cannot imagine any 'better' solution, and because we are so utterly incapable of making anything like it.

> "And then the kings stepped forth
> In all their might and power,
> Yet not one was there who could
> Set petal on a flower."

There are people who at this point will be feeling quite positive that that assertion is not true, for there are plenty of things in Nature which don't seem to us beautiful at all, but, on the contrary, quite hideous. Toads are seldom renowned for their beauty, and certain marine creatures look to us to be pretty revolting. But this comes from purely special circumstances. The toad has a face which reminds us of a fat and mis-shapen human face, and the deep-water fish reminds us of nothing at all. It, too, has been given that shape because it lives under conditions which are entirely different from those we know from personal experience. It quite simply seems foreign to us, and what is foreign often seems disquieting and unpleasant. If we make a distinction between ugly and beautiful, even where natural phenomena are concerned, it is because we are judging them from the view-point of our own experiences, dreams and ideals. In daily life it is not always easy to be completely unprejudiced and impartial in our judgments.

But it is one thing to enjoy the diversity of forms and compositions which Nature displays before our eyes, and

all Nature's forms are made with care and precision.

44

another to *make use of* them. We can go into raptures over a tree and the way the whole is built up, the exquisite manner in which all the transitions between stem, branches and twigs are accomplished. Yet if we try to put the various parts of a chair together in the same way, we would at once have a feeling that it was artificial and trashy. The thing is that we cannot get these parts really to grow out of each other, however badly we want to. Only God can do that. We have to do things the human way, making tenons and holes, using glue and screws. Then the whole thing will look right and no shame to us either.

If we wish to benefit by our experience of Nature, we must try to transpose the experience, the impressions it gives us. But before we start explaining how this can be done, we must first discover what it was which attracted our attention there, what it is we see in Nature. We shall discover that these are different things to those with which we were concerned when studying the cube.

CHARACTER

In the margin on the next page is a very simple little drawing. If you were asked what it represented you would unhesitatingly reply: a tree. But at the same time we can be quite sure that there isn't one tree in the whole world which looks just like that. Thus it is not a particular tree we have drawn, but a common notion of trees – a tree in general. We can also express this by saying that what we have drawn is something which has the *character* of a tree.

According to what we have already learned, we must almost call this tree formless. If we shut the book now, we would have great difficulty in reproducing either its main shape or its details. Yet we could easily draw something with the same character, the form of which is *like* a tree.

We are now using the word 'form' in quite a different

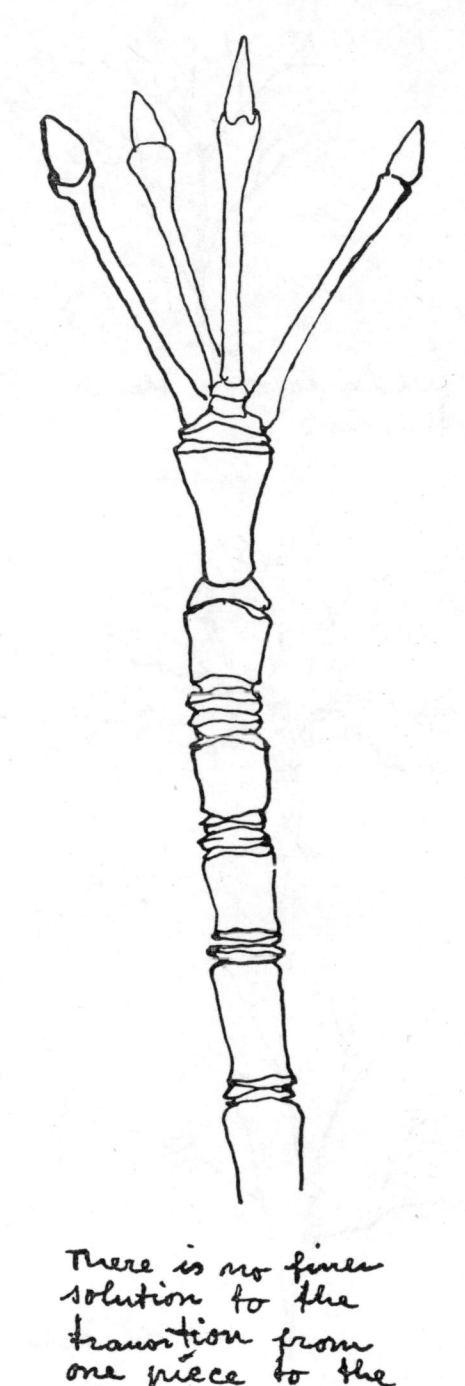

There is no finer solution to the transition from one piece to the other –

45

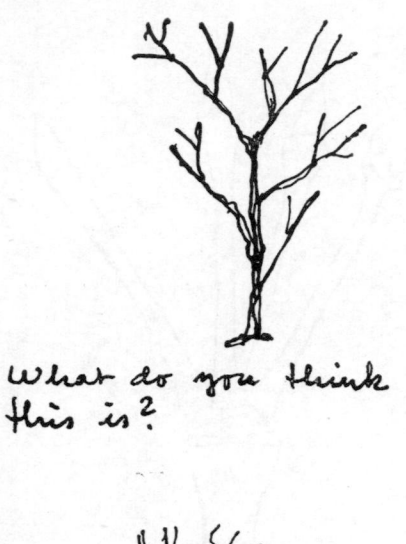

What do you think this is?

an oak.

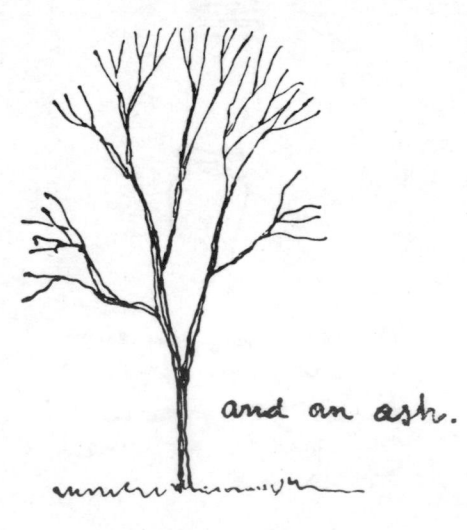

and an ash.

sense from that we have used hitherto, not to designate the whole or the outer contour, but to indicate special characteristics in the inner structure. If we were to try to explain these characteristics in words, we would have to say that the tree has a trunk, and that out from this trunk grow branches which themselves carry smaller branches and twigs. Again it is our *knowledge* of the concept 'tree' which makes it possible for us to apprehend and retain an experienced form.

We call forms of this kind *organic*. An organism means a *living unit*. Living, in contrast to the cube which was preeminently the dead, manufactured form. Our new understanding of form is thus associated not with the main form, but with the character of the organism.

Let us try to go deeper into this. We now draw two new trees, both of which have the same characteristics as the first which we described above. Yet none the less they are different, and we are entitled to say that the one is an oak, the other an ash. We can say that, because the branches on the two trees grow in the way characteristic of each and that is a thing which we can apprehend and reproduce – without having actual specimens of the two kinds of tree in front of us.

If we now take bits of the two drawings and put them together so that the ash tree gets oak branches, our reaction would be immediate. There's something wrong here, we would say. We could also strengthen the impression by making it more obvious; for example, by giving a palm tree fir branches. Even if we had never in our lives seen either a palm or a fir tree, we would still see that it was not right. This is because we have an instinct for natural forms – we see that something conflicts with Nature's order. We say that the phenomenon seems *inorganic*. We consider it ugly because it is impossible.

We can now try to apply what we have learned from Nature to an abstract form-phenomenon. We draw a line which bends and curves down the page. Yet for its whole

46

length the line is characterized by what seem to us to be related qualities, and remembering what we have just learned, we can perhaps say that it seems to be organic in nature. We now draw it again, but this time give it some abrupt kinks, which we are quite at liberty to do. We cannot get fir twigs to grow on palm trees, that is against the laws of Nature, but we can draw a line on a piece of paper exactly as we see fit. But all the same it looks as though we had sinned, done something illicit. The cohesion, the harmony is no longer there. The new line appears inorganic.

At last we can start on our real subject. On page 48 you can see a table which has two legs made of steel tubing and the other two of magnificent carved wood. We are at liberty to do even this, but we would also have the right to call it a really ugly table. It all seems quite pointless.

We have to use such crude examples if it is to be possible to illustrate the point in our small drawings. Nobody is likely to think of making that sort of thing; but it is an objection often made about houses that they seem inorganic. They don't look as though the different parts of them had the same origins, or were shaped by the same thought.

Later we shall be coming to style—a difficult and complex concept, so let it suffice here to state that one of the most important criteria for a thing having style, whether it dates from the present or the past, is that of the organic cohesion among its different parts. Not only should we have the feeling of the same material having been used throughout, but that this material has been shaped by the same tools, wielded by the same hand and guided by the same thought. The rococo chair on page 48 has nothing to do with Nature, yet we will still find in it some things characteristic of the plant or complex shell: a kind of unity of line, a relationship between its various parts, a cohesion in dimensions which stamps the whole as being something which has come about as a matter of course. That is how it

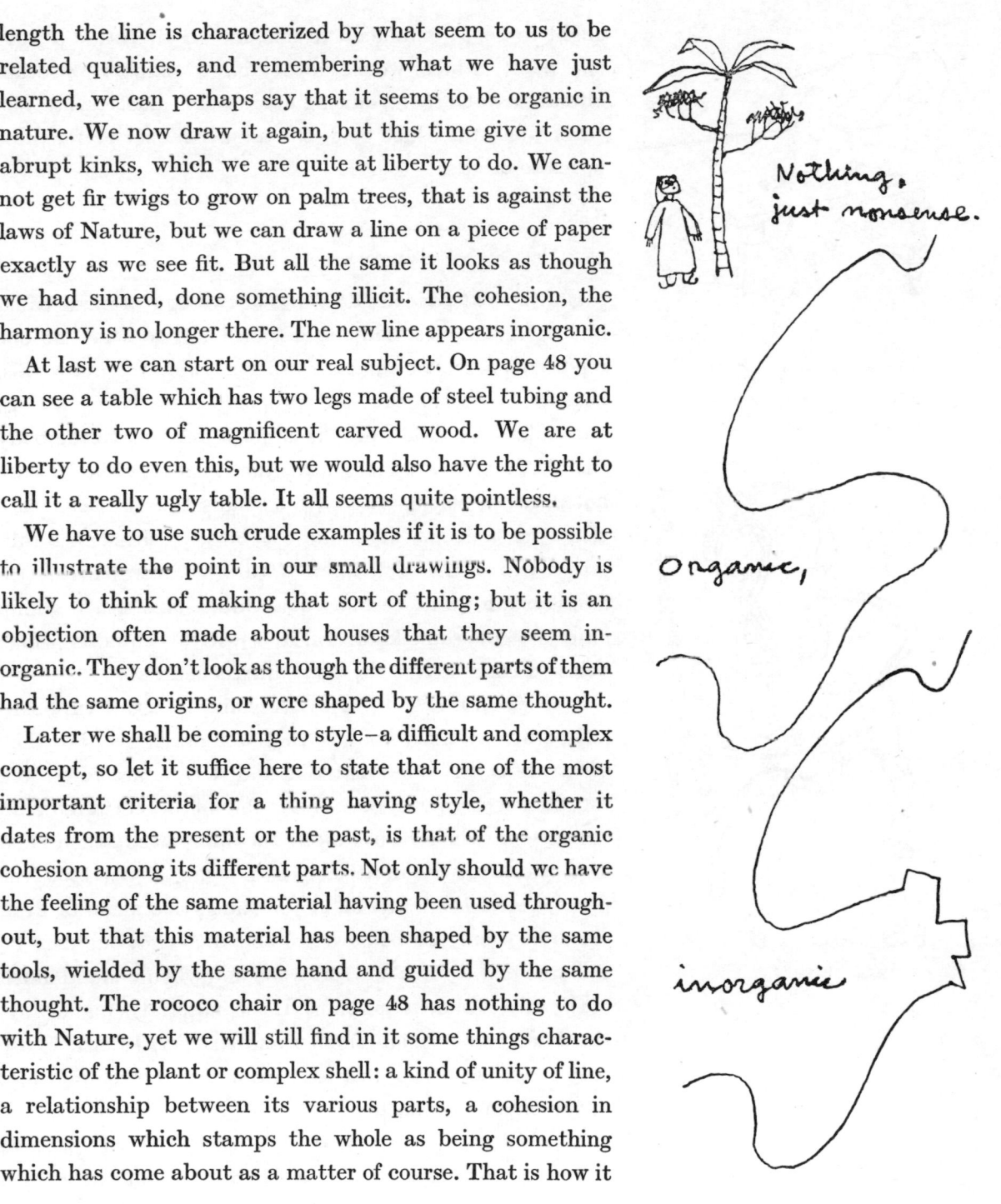

Nothing, just nonsense.

Organic,

inorganic

Something must be wrong here.

But here all is in order.

ought to be. It is difficult to imagine an alteration at any one point, which would not entail a number of other alterations at other points. Later on we must try to discover what it is which made the cabinet-maker prefer these forms to others.

EQUALITY OF DIMENSION

On the next page are drawings of two figures made equal in height. Despite that, no one will fail to see that one represents a grown man, the other a child. We know this, because something in the proportions tells us so. In particular, the child's head is larger in relation to the body than is the man's, which means that in reality the two are not far from being similar. On a young tree the leaves are all of the same size and almost as large as those on a full-grown tree of the same kind. Nature has seen fit to introduce certain units, certain equal dimensions which stamp objects of the same kind, and it is just this equality which helps to characterize the total difference in size.

This lesson is easy to apply. A chair and a tall cupboard have different dimensions, as they well may have; but they are made of the same material, and if they are to go well together we require that there should be certain detail dimensions, which recur despite the difference in their chief dimensions. These dimensions will again depend on the properties of the material. If the things are made of deal, the dimensions can be powerful and the edges ought to be well rounded, for deal is a soft wood and will not stand much in the way of knocks or bumps. If the material is mahogany, the detail can be made smaller and sharper. In either case they must be so executed that we notice the relationship, or the organic connection.

Another natural regulator we use when things have to have their dimensions fixed, is that they should fit in with our own measurements. That means that our chairs should be adjusted to the normal length of the body and that doors should be neither higher nor lower than a full-grown man can comfortably walk through. That is to say, they must be somewhat higher than the man, otherwise he won't feel safe. The door-handle must be placed to suit the hand. In this way a system of equal dimensions is introduced into both room and furniture which gives cohesion to the whole, just as did the leaves of equal size on the tree.

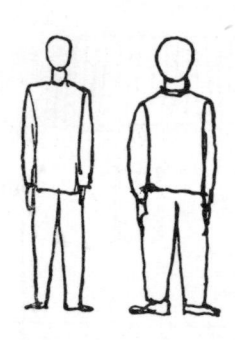

are these two really equally tall?

Not all ages, however, have held this view. In late eighteenth- and nineteenth-century houses you will often find doors which are nine feet high or more, and not only that but they may well be double doors. In those days it was thought that such oversize doors, which might have been made to admit processions with flags and brass bands, gave an added lustre and prestige to those who lived in the house. They also had the idea, inherited from earlier ages, that there should be a certain proportion between the size of doors and other details and that of the wall surfaces in which they were set. Today, however, we appear to think that the measure of an individual's importance should be looked for elsewhere. It is for the same reason, too, that we have stopped wearing ostrich plumes in our hats, and that sort of thing.

Higher door – greater dignity?

It is confusing if in a façade we set two windows with the same kind of division and the same proportion between height and breadth, but of different size. We cannot grasp that they belong to the same house. If there is to be any sense in the drawing of the two figures at the beginning of this section, we must take it that the two were viewed from different distances. Only in that way can they pictorially have the same height. There is very much the same effect with the two windows. In one way we realize that they are similar, and if there is a point of difference, it must be because the larger is nearer to us than the smaller. That is the effect they give, and this is why we become confused.

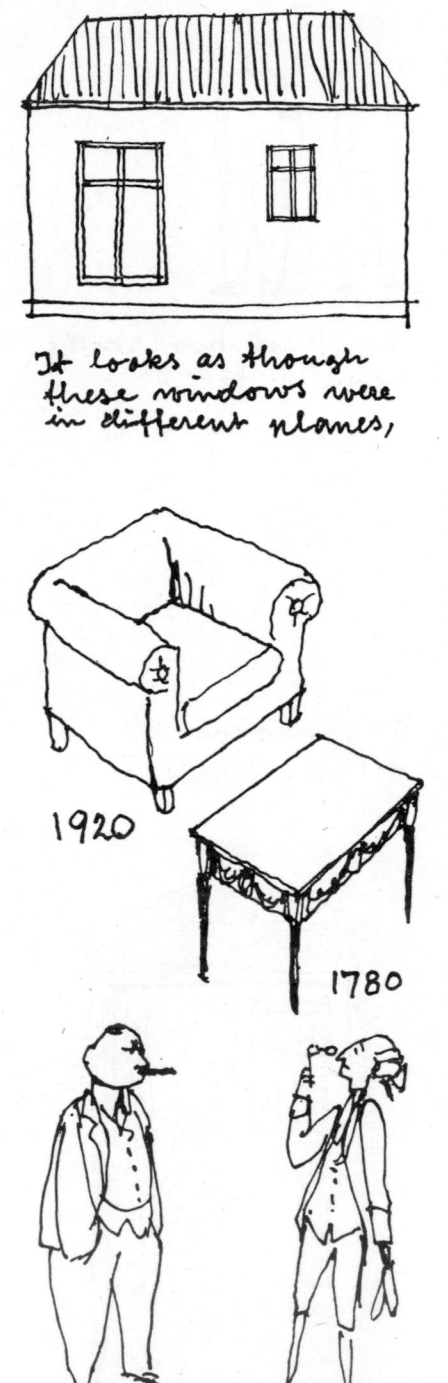

It looks as though these windows were in different planes,

1920

1780

That does not mean that all the windows in a façade should be of the same size. That could easily turn out stiff and boring and it would restrict the lay-out inside. But if they are to be different, there must be some advantage to it. Either that or they must have a division which permits the repetition of a common unit so that we have a point from which to use our yard-stick.

The basic rule for composing a pattern is very much the same. The whole must be built to the size of a certain unit, called a *module*, which governs the character and size of the entire composition. In the case of an embroidery, we let the technical aspect be the determining factor. If it is to be done in cross-stitch, that gives us the unit straight away, and no one, it is to be hoped, would think of combining cross-stitch with broad-stitch. That would at once give us two heterogeneous scales, and there would be no knowing which we were to go by.

One question which can be asked in this connection, and which is frequently heard, is to what degree it is 'permissible' to put things from different periods together in the same room. As a rule it will be a question here of things which are different in character and expression, and as such it is mostly difficult to give a general answer, for it all depends on what the things look like. But, at any rate, you can think of many examples where such combinations will not only 'do', but where the objects concerned will show each other up to advantage. If we have some nice rococo chairs, but lack a table, it would be better to get an ordinary modern table which is simple and good, rather than have a new rococo table made to 'go with' them. Experience shows that it is almost never worth making copies of old things in order that they seem convincing, and, besides, there is little joy in just copying what others have done before. It is far better to make something for ourselves, something which will suit us and our age. All the same, it is perfectly possible to achieve good cohesion in such groups as long as we take care that the different dimensions are of the same or related character.

CHEAP CONSTRUCTIONS

The proverb tells us that it is not worth catching at straws, they are so paltry and unserviceable. But straws have their own mission to fulfil. Out in the field they carry their heavy heads, slender and tall and erect. And when a gust of wind comes, they all billow like a stormy sea, yet it takes a lot to break them, thin as they are. In other words, they must be especially finely made. If we cut one through, we will see that it is hollow. All the 'bearing elements', as they are called in the language of builders, consist of fibres arranged as a tube. By this means the maximum strength is achieved in relation to the amount of material used.

The wild chervil also has a tubular stem. If we cut it through we can distinctly see how it is built up of various elements: the plant-flesh which forms the bearing parts, and strong fibres which act as a sort of armour, or stiffening to stop it bending. The fibres are set in a ring, and the flesh fits tightly round them so as to form grooves on the outside of the stalk. Thereby, too, the stalk's construction is illustrated in its external form. It has often been asserted that it was from this plant the Greeks copied the fluting on their temple pillars. There is no knowing about that, but there is probably some connection. At all events the raised parts caused by the fluting give an impression of rigidity and strength.

There is no doubt that our conception of beautiful construction coincides with Nature's own systems. Here we do not regard economy as a virtue of necessity, but as an end in itself. But in this connection economy does not mean the fact of costing less in shillings and pence. That would depend on a number of fortuitous factors such as changes in the prices

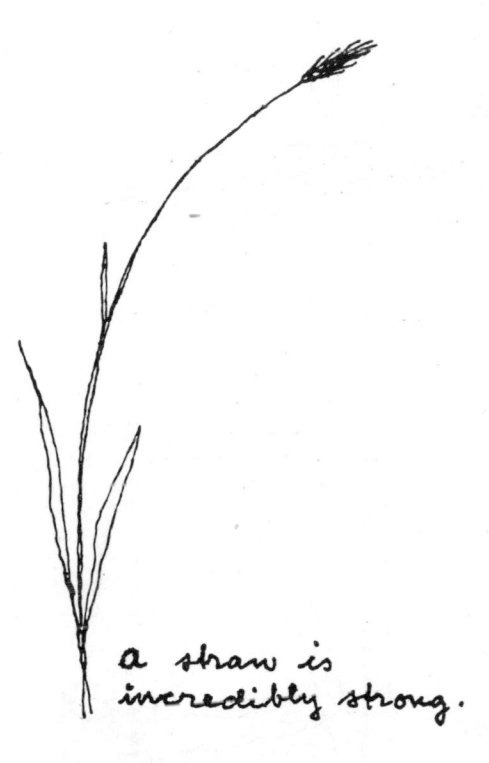

a straw is incredibly strong.

Section of a grooved flower stalk.

51

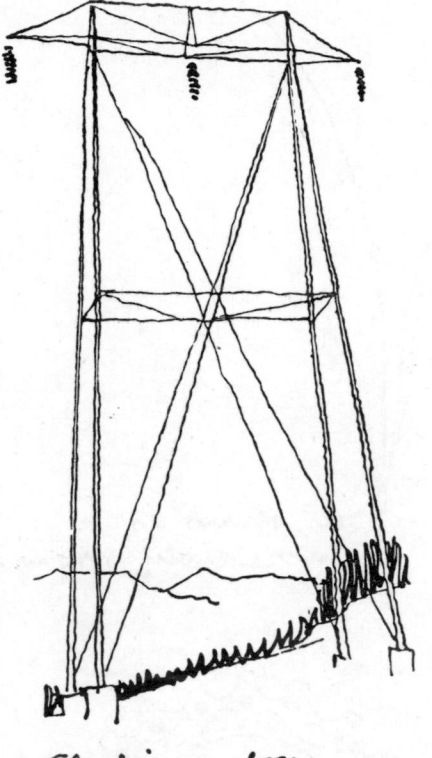

Electric pylon.
Maximum of strength
for the minimum
of material.

of materials, of wage rates and methods of procedure. Nor can we say that it is the construction using the least amount of material, which appears to be the lightest, which is the most beautiful. That proposition is only true when it concerns articles of unequivocably constructive character.

A drop of water on a table-top has a special shape, just as a drop of water is a concept with a special magnitude, i.e. that volume which the thin surface film is able to hold together. When the drop is lying on a table, this film is stretched to the uttermost and the contents will assume such a shape that the pressure on the film will be equal everywhere. We consider such a constructive form to be beautiful because it is perfect.

In the course of the centuries engineers have learned how to calculate the strength of the various forms of construction, so that they could be made just as strong as was required. After that we were not so interested in what seemed most right to the eye, or in the lessons of Nature; but then to our great surprise we discovered that the computations often coincided with specific natural phenomena. But, really, there is nothing very strange in that, for the same powers direct it all.

But we must not let that beguile us into thinking, as certain engineers seem to do, that a form is beautiful because it is the result of accurate computations. Before you can compute, you must have a point of departure; thus, what is decisive for the final result is whether or not that point of departure was correctly chosen; for this, intuition is required and an intelligent constructive faculty. Thus Nature can still play a part as source of inspiration.

GOOD PROPORTIONS

When we say that a tree is beautiful, that has nothing to do with the proportion of its height to its breadth. A low, spreading oak can be as lovely as a tall, slender poplar. What matters is its character and inner qualities, not its *proportions*. It is only when we come to use it in a composition in conjunction with forms of landscape and houses that we will start thinking whether we prefer one form to the other.

And it is not much we expect of trees, only that they shall be there growing. They must have roots to extract nourishment and keep them fixed to the hillside, a trunk with branches and twigs with leaves, and they must be strong enough to bear their own weight. And that is just how strong they are. Otherwise they do not have to do anything which would make more complex demands on their structure and performance.

Live animals have many more tasks to fulfil than have the stationary plants which so far we have taken as our examples. They have to be able to run about, swim or fly, as well as to get themselves food in different ways. As has already been said, we cannot help preferring some animals to others, as they have qualities which we admire to a greater or lesser extent, or perhaps even envy.

The salmon and the mackerel have been proclaimed two of the most beautiful of all fish, because they are such phenomenal swimmers. The eagle is the king among birds, because it combines great skill at flying with great strength of beak and talons. But such birds as swallows and seagulls also come high up the list because of their graceful and assured flight. Where the quadrupeds are concerned, it is those who are both strong and swift whom we place at the top—the lions and tigers. But speed by itself is also an enviable quality, and thus the antelope, the fallow-deer and the stag also have a place in our hearts, to say nothing of the horse which puts its abilities at our service. All these have qualities which we would like to possess, and therefore throughout the ages they have been used as comparisons in vaunting our own or other people's skill or proficiency.

The eagle is the king of birds.

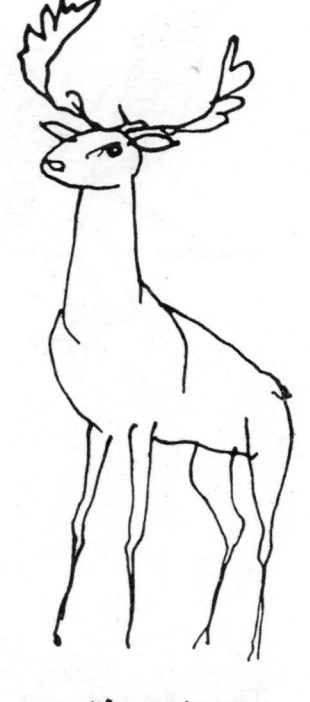

To us the stag's lines symbolize all that is swift and graceful

With such creatures the proportion between body and head, between height and length, between the shapes of the different limbs, ceases to be a thing of no importance. We assess it all by the yard-stick of what we call being *well made*, which is a very precise concept as far as the different species are concerned, as you quickly realize when you watch the judges at a horse show. The sum of our experience of the well-made or shapely can itself be condensed as being our view of the *normal* in the world of our fellow creatures, and that view determines what we instinctively prefer. The dachshund is excellently made for hunting in tunnels underground, but up on the surface it looks rather comical with its long body and short legs. There is a very definite connection between the giraffe's long neck and the food it prefers, and it is an experience to see it galloping. Yet we still feel that on the whole it is rather exaggerated.

Pride of place among creatures we give to ourselves, our own bodies. This could appear both conceited and extraordinary considering how deficient our body is. Even though some people are said to swim like a fish or to be as strong as a lion, that is not accurate. And we certainly cannot fly. But we combine in ourselves *more* qualities than any animal, and we use them for our conscious purposes. And in judging the human body we have developed a sense of proportion which is incredibly sharp. A man to whom it would never occur to express an opinion about the proportions of a chair or a cupboard, will not hesitate to pronounce the ears of some chance person to be big, his legs long or neck short, even though the deviation from normal may only be very slight.

We often use direct comparisons from the human body in describing things. We can call a jug pot-bellied and thereby conjure up a festive association, just as there often is something festive about a man whom much good food has rendered pot-bellied. But we can also express disapproval and say that it has flabby lines, and then it is of an obese person we think.

It is also possible to establish harmony between forms, and also a feeling of purely physical stress and movement. Contemplation of an object can cause purely physical reactions and their accompanying sensations. We often speak of a *resilient* curve, when its shape in one way or another reminds us of a leg, an arm or a whole body in a tensed attitude, while at the same time giving a feeling of concentrated strength. We may well think that a tall, slender vase is stretching its neck and that again will mean that it gives the impression of nervous watchfulness, perhaps also of refinement. In a building, low protruding side-wings can give the impression of embracing arms, the expression used by the great seventeenth-century architect, Bernini, when he was explaining the idea of the colonnades of St. Peter's. All these are means which the creator of form will employ quite spontaneously when he wishes to give his work a certain meaning or attitude.

Equally important and decisive for our feeling for form is the fact that the human body, together with the ideal animal forms, has given us established feelings for certain main proportions. These are to be found in the architecture and handicrafts of all ages. Sometimes they have been used consciously; at other times they are the result of spontaneous feeling for the connection between things. They are also to be found as abstractions, translated into purely mathematical formulae. We then discover how the ideal geometrical forms, such as the cube, coincide with those other forms which have their roots in Nature. The experts often quarrel about what was the point of departure, but there is no need for us to enter their debate. It is better that we should marvel at, and be glad, that the various concepts and notions can be of composite origin, and yet have the same basic aims.

Utensil with human simi-larity

Nor is there really any need to produce a number of examples, but here is one which clearly illustrates what we are discussing and which has greatly occupied the theorists for many centuries. This is the doctrine of

THE GOLDEN SECTION

If we want to divide the erect human body with a horizontal line in such a way as to emphasize its character, most of us would choose to draw our line through the waist. It will be noticed that we haven't done anything subtle or elaborate, but just taken what seems to be the obvious course. This has given us three different measurements: A, which represents the body's full height; B, which is the height from the soles of its feet to the waist; and C, the height from the waist to the top of the head. If we take these measurements in centimetres and look to see if we can find a numerical connection between them, we will find that there is one. They can be put together in this formula:

$$A : B = B : C$$

Or, to put it another way: the whole height is to the larger part what the larger part is to the smaller. Or we can say that the larger part is the mean proportional between the whole and the smaller part.

If we want to express this in an abstract form, we can make a rectangle in which A and B are the length of the sides. If we examine this rectangle we will discover that it has a remarkable property: we cannot call it short or compressed, nor can we say that it is specially elongated; but if we put a piece of tracing paper over it and start experimenting with a pencil, we will find that the height cannot be altered without entirely destroying the character of the rectangle. In its own way it is almost as fixed in its proportions as the square, yet the proportion between the sides

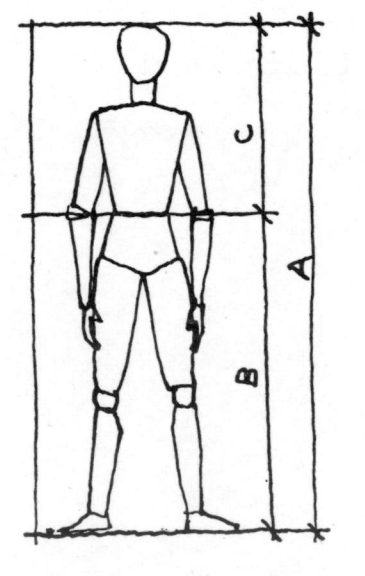

The human body and the golden section.

is far more complicated. We have before us the famous *proportion of the Golden Section.*

Many people have accepted this proportion as something divine, a revelation, and insist that we stick to it. Others are not so dogmatic and regard it as *convenient*, beautiful, but no more.

The geometrical formula itself goes back to the Greek mathematicians, but we do not find it used as a conscious element in architectural compositions until the Renaissance. In our day the famous French architect, Le Corbusier, has been its ardent advocate, and, latterly, many have tried to show also that it has been used in the architecture both of antiquity and of the Middle Ages. Many of the supporting analyses seem convincing, though others appear forced. There are so many ways of measuring. But if all this has shown that the numerical and visual requirements coincide, that is a thing of importance.

DIMENSIONS OF THE BODY

It is not only the proportions of our bodies which count in our consciousness, but obviously also their absolute measurements. This is all dealt with in another connection, but even so it is a subject which requires its own little section.

Originally all peoples calculated in measures which corresponded directly with different parts of our bodies. The smallest measure was the breadth of a thumb (an *inch*); then came the length of a *foot*. We used to have a *yard*, roughly the length of an arm, and finally there is the *fathom* or what one can embrace. In the early stages of development we simply made direct use of the part of the body concerned, but later, of course, definite measures were set up – prototypes. The rule became twelve inches to a foot, three feet to a yard, and so on. That it was possible to get these magnitudes to fit so nicely, hints that

A (B)

B (C)

The golden section.

57

it has also been possible to discover a connection between the human body and the world of numerals.

These units were clumsy to work with, yet they had the great advantage that they referred to something with which we were familiar. A measurement given in feet is a body's measurement, there is something right and familiar about it. To make calculations easier, most European countries have now gone over to the *metre* and the units above and below which go with it and at which we arrive by dividing or multiplying by ten. The metre itself is an (inaccurate) fraction of the earth's circumference, and to whom does that convey anything? We are not going to try and put that right, but just to point out that in architecture and hand-crafts the body's measurements still provide the point of departure for our appreciation.

Few people will know how many centimetres a cup with a handle measures, but we can all see with half an eye if it is too large to hold or if the handle is too small. To mark off two metres along a wall is not easy until we remember that that is the length of a bed–the length of the body with a little bit extra at either end.

When all the furniture in a room is related to the measurements of the human body, it becomes like an instrument with all its strings tuned to the same keynote. However obvious and easy to follow this may seem, it is strangely enough one of the spheres in which we still sin wholesale. It is true that we have got the height of doors and ceilings down to reasonable proportions, but it is nothing unusual to find arm-chairs which appear to have been designed more for elephants than for humans. That is supposed to give an impression of prosperity. The coffee cups displayed on the side-table of such a room go to the other extreme and are so small that you cannot hold them, and the amount of coffee they contain is negligible. They are supposed to be elegant. The bookshelves are down by the floor so that you

For whom was this chair made – people or elephants?

have to get down on hands and knees to read the titles, and the lamps either hang close under the ceiling or stand on low tables, so that nowhere is there a good light by which to read or work.

To all this must be added an inexplicable urge to fill up the room with all sorts of unnecessary bits and pieces, a thing which strangely enough is associated with the notion of comfort. This again is another sin against the needs of the body; for the body requires a certain freedom of movement, just as much as it wants to rest when the time comes for that. Of such rooms we say that they haven't room to swing a cat. It is not that we are sadists and wish to do that; but we like to feel that we can at least swing our arms about if we want to. That describes the space the body feels that it needs. We can easily illustrate this by taking up position facing a wall with a piece of chalk in either hand and making a mark at the limits of our reach in either direction. That gives something which means something. Similarly, we feel that we want to be able to walk about even when indoors. It is not a question of a proper walk, but of being able to take enough steps for the body to be moving in its natural rhythm.

You would think that it was easy enough to arrive at the dimensions of furniture best suited to the human body. But strangely enough it is not. Faced with a ceremonial chair from the end of the seventeenth century, most people would say that it was awful. The seat is both too shallow and too high; the back is narrow and far too straight up-and-down. Many people imagine that the cabinet-makers of those days knew no better; that the comfortable type of chair of our day had not yet been invented. No, it wasn't because of that, but because no one bothered very much about comfort as we know it. People then had other needs, and a different attitude to life from our own.

Perhaps, too, we have acquired a better knowledge of

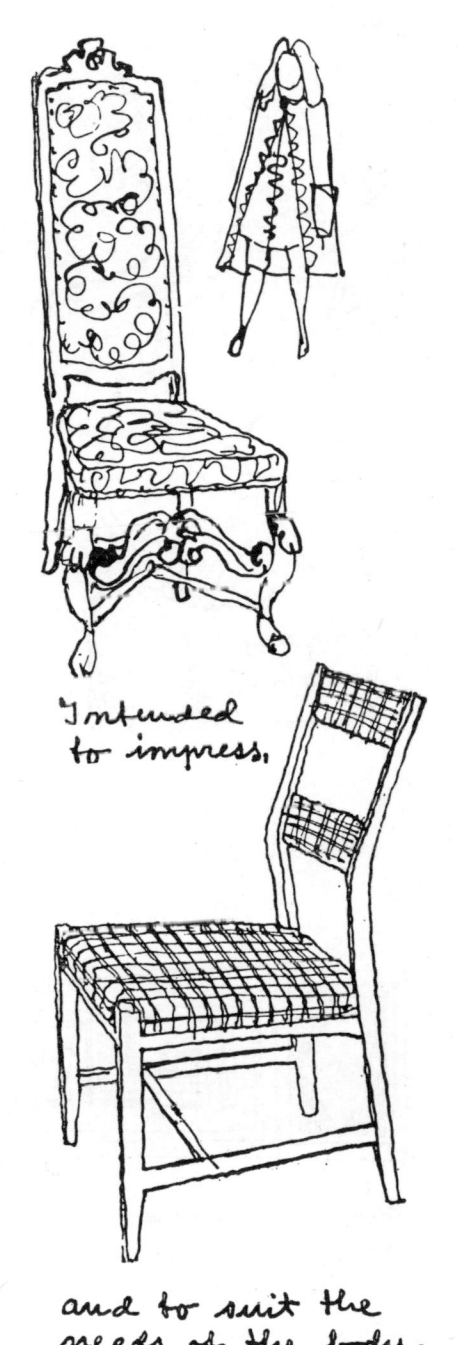

Intended to impress,

and to suit the needs of the body.

59

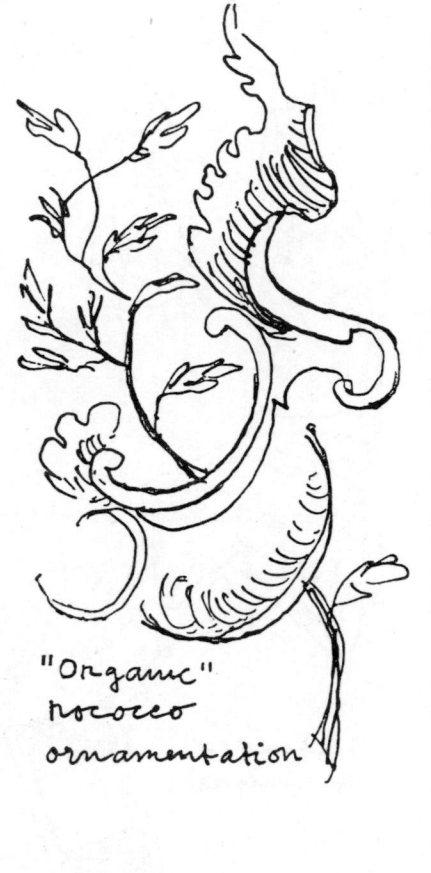

"Organic"
rococo
ornamentation

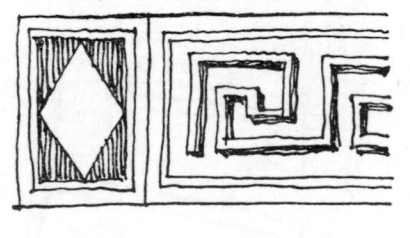

Empire geometrical
ornamentation.

these things in recent years. Medical science has learned a lot more of our physical needs, and our desire for health, to have a well-cared-for body, has increased correspondingly. Yet even though they now have this direct approach, people still have difficulty in making their own observations, as the following example shows:

Some years ago an investigation was made in Oslo in which a number of housewives were asked, among other things, whether the height of the work-tables in their kitchens suited them. Almost all replied that they did, that they were all right. This surprised the architects, who thought they were too low. They then asked the housewives if they often had pains in their backs, and to that they also answered "Yes", at any rate the older ones. Yet it had never occurred to them that the two things might be connected.

NOW WE KNOW MORE ABOUT FORM

Let us try to summarize what we have learned so far. We have seen that we can appreciate form and shape in two different ways. The first was entirely a matter of mental activity, of the way the eye worked, both things which to us appeared to be independent of outside experience. We will call this type of form, which is so to speak the most severe, *formal*. Certain periods, such as the Empire in the first half of the nineteenth century, have one-sidedly culti-vated this aspect of the matter. Their buildings were made up of pure rectangular or cylindrical blocks with flat wall surfaces and geometrical ornamentation.

The second attitude relies on impulses from the world of natural form, the animal and vegetable kingdoms. Here it is pre-eminently the character of the detail which is striking, in connection with its organic structure. This province of form also ought to have a name and it would surely be correct to call it the *organic*.

60

Here, too, we discovered impulses which supported our notions of proportions based on laws and, in this sphere, we found a connection between formal concepts and those where the stress was organic.

The rococo chair made an excellent illustration of the organic conception of form; it was the character of the individual parts which we first noticed—the external contour is more difficult to comprehend. We must remember, though, that the examples sketched here are very special. In the great majority of man's creations both views will be represented at the same time.

There is still another way of looking at things, which has a great effect on our experience of form and which so far we have only just mentioned. This is that where consideration for the *use* of a thing, for its *utility*, enters into it. This requires a chapter to itself.

Albrecht Dürer's Melancholia (1514) pondering among other things the problem of form.

CHAPTER FOUR

Which is concerned with tools and things we use, and of the connection between form and function.

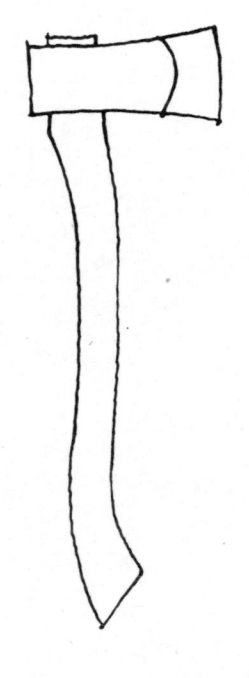

The axe is a good and well-shaped tool.

The thing depicted here is not made in accordance with geometric notions which the mind can apprehend. It would be difficult to find it a place in a comprehensible mathematical system, and the eye draws no auxiliary lines to help integrate it. Nor does it remind us of anything we know in Nature; there are no characteristic features linking its two principal parts. None the less, we are entirely familiar with it, and if we regard it with an open and unbiased eye we will discover that it is beautiful. For it, too, is perfect in its way. The sight of this shape arouses many an emotion, for we know very well what it represents. It is an axe, and it tells us that it is made to chop with.

No one person shaped the axe; it is the outcome neither of personal taste nor of desires, but the sum of experiences which are themselves the result of trying to get it as suited to its purpose as possible. We can make the old test of closing the book and seeing if we can draw what we have just seen: the result will undoubtedly be quite right. If we don't quite remember what the model looked like, we can shut our eyes again, and *feel* its shape in our hands. For it is just there that most of our experience of axes lies.

We call the axe a *tool*, something we have constructed to extend the scope of what our limbs are able to accomplish. Our idea of it is of a shape, because here, too, we have a special knowledge, that is, of its functional suitability. When it is stuck in the chopping-block, it is a dead thing, but as soon as we take it in our hand, it forms a sort of extension of our arm, so that we can reach farther and can strike harder. And the actual blade of the axe becomes like a new hand, not so delicate as our own, but considerably more suitable for splitting logs.

A tool we generally regard as being a thing used in connection with work, but fundamentally we can include *everything* we have around us in the same category. It is tools which give us greater possibilities in all spheres. Clothes enhance the ability of our skin to withstand cold, and a hat protects our faces from sun and rain better than the thickest mop of hair. If we sit on the floor it may not be easy to get up quickly, so it is better to have an instrument for sitting—a chair. This we can regard as a pair of artificial legs which enables us to assume other postures than those which the structure of our bodies by itself permits. The back on a chair acts as a reinforcement for our own spine which we could often wish more solid. The cooking stove in the kitchen is a tool which enables us to eat things which our teeth and stomach cannot deal with alone. Even the shelf on the wall is of direct assistance to the body. On it we can put the things we want to get at quickly and so don't need to carry them continually in our hands. The most important of all kinds of tool are the houses in which we live—there is no end to the help and assistance they give us. And if we take a look round the room in which we are sitting we will not find a thing which is not a tool, at least originally, unless it is the flowers in the vase (if there are any), or a picture on the wall. (Yet many people consider that our urge to make pictures had a definite purpose in the beginning, a purely magical one.)

In their simplest form all these aids are simple everyday affairs. They were not made as the result of observation of nature, or of profound meditation on the essence of form.

Good tools have their own refined beauty.

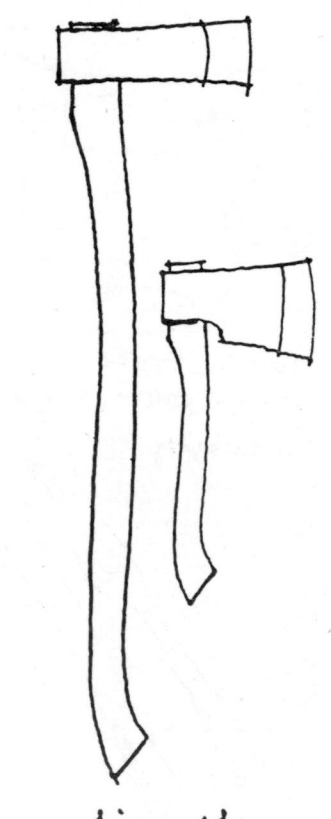

a question of
proportions?
No, of different
uses.

None the less we love them well, for they constitute an extension of ourselves, the means we use to improve our lot, to dominate Nature which gives us nothing unless we help ourselves; or to satisfy the demands that the complications of civilized life make upon us. For the strange thing about human beings is that they are almost worse equipped to get along on their own than any other creature. It is our ability to fashion ourselves tools that has brought us to the top, and as our development has progressed, we have grown more and more dependent on them. So, it is obvious that we also set store by our tools, and take joy in the forms and shapes which we between us have given them.

(Many sculptors give their works the form of jars and pots, of utensils, though it is by no means the intention that they should ever be used. This is an obvious example of how attached we are to those things, how we wrap them round with notions which the artist knows he would otherwise have difficulty in conveying.)

As I have said, it is always what we know about things which makes it possible for us to comprehend and grasp their form. If an axe has a longer or shorter haft, we don't now wonder whether the haft has the right proportions in regard to the size of the head; what we think of is whether the haft suits the weight of the head, whether it is a timber axe or one for chopping firewood. When we see a chair, our first thought is whether it is comfortable to sit on. That is to say, we don't actually *think* that, we feel it with our whole bodies as a purely instinctive reaction. If its seat is covered with brocade and its legs carved, that may possibly be a further asset; but, whatever it is, we will require that all decoration and adornment be kept sufficiently in check for the actual mission and purpose of the chair to be neither scamped nor camouflaged.

Are the utilitarian forms always beautiful in themselves? That is a question which has occupied many people in modern times, when economic considerations have largely forced us to work with such forms without the addition of decoration, and when we have had little chance of making our houses and our furniture satisfy the more purely *formal* requirements. Before answering, let us first take a look at some specifically utilitarian objects about whose beauty of shape we shall easily agree, and see if they can help us to see our way clearly.

The axe is beautiful in its simple way. Skis have a shape and line which the eye delights to follow, but it is best of all to look at them when they are on your feet and gliding through the snow. A sailing boat, a proper racing yacht, is to many one of the loveliest things imaginable, especially when it is sailing in a wind of just that strength for which it was designed to give its best performance. A fighter aeroplane in the air is one of the most perfect things man's hands have fashioned, at any rate as far as obvious function and efficiency are concerned.

All these are instruments intended to be in motion or at least driven by hand or foot. But we can also find examples among stationary objects, such as a bridge. Whether it is a rural bridge of stone or a modern concrete structure with an impressive span, it is beautiful if we have the feeling that the material has been rightly used and proper advantage taken of its qualities. A bathroom with its porcelain, glazed tiles and chromed metal, telling of water and cleanliness and hygienic conditions, also has a beauty of its own, which is most evident when no attempt has been made to deck it out.

INDETERMINATE FUNCTIONS

However different all these examples may appear, they all have one thing in common: the purpose they were to fulfil is exceptionally clear, understandable and un-ambiguous. The axe had *only* to chop, and we all know what that is. The skis were *only* to take us easily across the snow. The sailing boat and the aeroplane were both to

Everyone sees beauty in a sailing boat,

and in an aeroplane.

Suspension bridge.
Functional = beautiful.

travel as fast as possible each in its element, and we were careful to select examples where no attention was paid to the comfort of passengers or to other subordinate aspects. The bridge and the bath also had each a simple and obvious mission to perform.

Let us take the chair we mentioned a short while ago. Sitting is also quite a definite thing, though it is by no means uniform. We like to sit high when we eat, lower when we read and lower still when we want to rest. What chair then are we to regard as the most suitable: that which can be used for a little of each, or the three which are specially made each for its own purpose?

The very construction, the way the chair is made, is itself a complex problem. The bridge we mentioned has to support a certain load of people and vehicles crossing it, it is no more complicated than that. It is the load, too, which is the main thing in the construction of a chair, yet it also has to be able to stand up to a little rocking backwards and forwards. It must also be able to be lifted or pushed about a room, and preferably without leaving marks on the floor or walls when this is done. It is no great matter to find a construction that will stand up to all this, but it is quite impossible to find one which expresses, which *obviously shows that especial attention has been paid to each separate function*. And then there is another question: do we like it to be one hundred per cent adapted to its purpose, that is to say, designed for a special position (and body)?

Imagine a man who has discovered that at his desk he likes to sit just so. In order to get a chair that really suits him, he has a cast made of his body bent at just the angle he likes. From the cast a steel plate is pressed and then mounted on a stand of light construction. There he has his functional chair, yet he will not be able to endure sitting in it for very long at a time; because, in a chair, we also like to be able to move, to shift a bit, cross one leg over the other. We can think of plenty of other ways of solving that problem of construction, but there can be only *one* haft for the timber-axe.

Then let us imagine a modern machine, for example a printing machine. It is entirely adapted to its purpose—several generations of ingenious engineers have done their best to make it as simple and efficient as possible. Is it beautiful? We cannot claim outright that it is. In the first place there is no doubt that its main shape could have been fashioned in many other ways, and in the second place we do not *know*, as a matter of course, how it actually does its work. We have already decided on several occasions that our appreciation of form depends on what we know of the thing, on our understanding its logic, whether this is theoretical or practical. This does not mean that the printing machine may not have other qualities which make it beautiful, and in any event it is very entertaining to see it at work.

The examples allow us to come to a far-reaching conclusion: *a form that is adapted to its purpose is synonymous with a beautiful form as long as we are concerned with clear, obvious and uncomplicated considerations*. This rule, however, ceases to hold as soon as we begin demanding versatility in use and the possibility of different constructions. But this does not prevent regard for a thing's serviceableness always being the basic consideration and the decisive one in the fashioning of all objects which really are made to be used for something and not just to be looked at. We want things to be fashioned correctly for their use, so long as that use can be gauged.

This view has prevailed in all ages. But it is not always so easy to discern when we come to the historical things. As we have already mentioned, our idea of what is serviceable, or of the way to use things, has varied. And it is also possible for things to be fashioned in such a way that it is their other qualities which first catch the eye. The rococo

Functional chair?

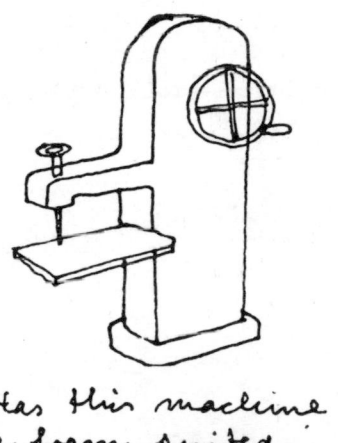

Has this machine a form suited to its purpose? We cannot know!

chair, illustrated farther back, is a perfectly serviceable chair, suitable in its measurements, pleasant to sit in; yet the first thing we notice about it is its luxuriant decoration. Our own age is so occupied with purpose and function that we dislike cluttering up with ornamentation and fuss the appearance of a thing meant for use. On this basis we developed in the 1920s and 1930s a style of our own which we have called *functionalism*.

Beautiful or not beautiful is often a question of what is meant by the word 'beautiful'. We can at least agree that it is always *pleasing* when things appear to be just right. An old worn-out countrywoman, nice and kindly but with a wrinkled face and old clothes, is not beautiful when compared with a film star, but she is pleasing, because she is thoroughly *genuine* and perhaps many of us would get on better with her than with the film star.

The beautiful against the pleasing

CONSTRUCTION AND TECHNIQUE

When we have to build a bridge, we do not wish to use more material than is strictly necessary. To do otherwise is to throw money away. The more we can find out about the way the various forces and loads affect construction, the more we can save by using materials in the correct dimensions. And the more beautiful the structure seems to us to be—with the reservations mentioned above.

In the same way we think a table ugly if its legs are thicker than they need be. We think then that it is clumsy, or that it is trying to make itself heavier and more important than it is. And if instead of four legs it has a stand which has no connection with sensible construction, then we consider it pointless and unpleasant. We do not know, cannot see why the carpenter gave the underframe that form and shape. And because of that it is difficult to understand and there is no *form*.

FORM AND MATERIAL

Before we can know whether these table-legs have suitable dimensions, we must know a little about the material of which they are made. And that is just what we do. We do not need to be craftsmen, not even especially clever with our hands, to have that knowledge. Every day we take hundreds of different things in our hands, and even a person who spends most of his time at a desk in a government office, has as a child cut a willow pipe, bent wire and hammered in nails. In this way we have got ourselves a store of knowledge which is larger than most of us realize. And because of it we know immediately that an underframe of steel-tubing can and *should* be slighter than one of wood. If it is a question of choosing between different kinds of wood, we know, too, that deal is not as strong as oak or mahogany, and that deal accordingly calls for larger dimensions. For the same reason things made of that wood require a softer form. (Compare this with what we said of the hard cube and the soft ball.)

We must mention several other examples in order properly to realize how decisive this aspect of our form-perception is. Let us look at a ceramic dish. It is formed in soft clay which is then baked and glazed. That makes the material hard, but also rather brittle. All these qualities mean that the article must be fairly thick, and it will last even longer if the exposed upper edge is made fairly stout. Its round shape is the natural one for the brittle material, for it is then strongest and has no vulnerable corners. But it is also a matter of course, because the plate was made on a wheel, where the soft lump of clay turned round and round between the hands shaping it. Let us assume that we consider this a good and proper shape.

The same shape, however, will appear ugly and pointless if it is made in silver. Silver is both hard and tough, and it

Handmade glass. (Tough supple mass)

Handmade silver (Tough and hard) —

and handmade earthenware (soft)

Chair of steel tubing
and pressed laminated
wood.
New technique —
new form.

clear construction,
organic cohesion
a beautiful chair.

has no need of the same dimensions. And the way of making a silver plate is quite different. Silver objects are usually pressed or hammered out of flat plates.

Thus not only the material, but also the way of manufacture has something to say when we are making up our minds whether a shape is good or bad. And not even here does the ordinary person require any special professional knowledge. As a general rule he can safely rely on his sensibility, though it may often be necessary to show him that he actually has that sensibility and ought to rely on it. When he realizes this he will have more right to express an opinion on what is ugly or lovely.

NOW WE KNOW STILL MORE ABOUT WHAT FORM IS

Once again we had better sum up what we know, so as to be quite clear what it is we have learned. Early we decided that there were *two* backgrounds to our experience of form, one formal and the other organic. To these two groups we can now add a third, that which is based on the idea of the *functional*. That also brings us to the end of this analysis. It must be pointed out that such divisions are necessarily fairly rough and schematic. There are many things the form and appearance of which give us pleasure without our being able to explain exactly why, and many of you may still think that such attempted elucidations are boring and pointless. Such must just be referred to the introduction, where it was said that increased knowledge and understanding will in the long run lead to increased pleasure and clearer perception.

Nor can one say that this analysis of ideas is in any way artificial. As we have seen, we can find many things whose form belongs to just the one of these groups. As often as not, however, the notions will be interwoven, even though one of them may predominate. Let us now investigate what it is that makes us attach greatest weight to this or that factor.

CHAPTER FIVE

Which deals with the interpretation of beauty and ugliness, and what we mean by the word style.

We must still stand by our basic principle: that appreciation of form depends on what we know of things. If the form agrees with what we know, so that we get a complete and clear impression, we call it *beautiful*. If it runs counter to our ideas of the essence of the thing, we call it *ugly*. Ugly, or at any rate *without interest*, we might say, if it represents something we don't know or have no knowledge of.

Beauty and ugliness are thus relative ideas. Opinions about them can change from one generation to another or differ from country to country, between different strata of society, in accordance with differences in knowledge, interpretation and perception. In the eighteenth century, people considered the architecture of the Middle Ages primitive and barbaric, it did not in the least fit in with the period's opinion of the things that mattered. If our age holds a different view, it must be because we *know* more about the people of the Middle Ages, or that our attitude coincides with theirs on many points. It would be wrong for us to say that the people of the baroque age had no sense of beauty because they did not like Gothic. We can, however, say that they were rather one-track or narrow-minded in their attitude to life, or that their knowledge of history was not as good as it could have been.

From this again it follows that a limitation in our

Baroque would not see the beauty in a building like this.

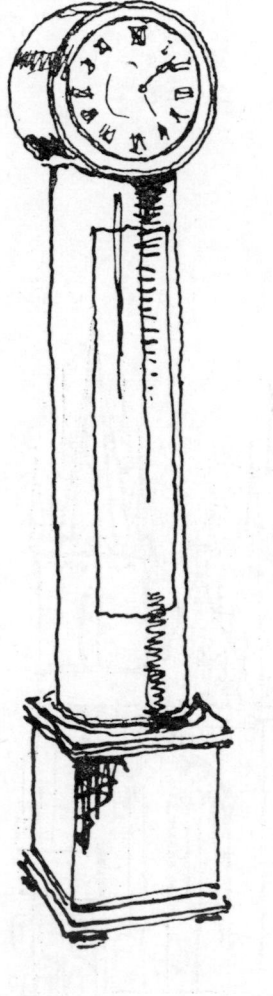

Clock composed of
two cylinders and
a cube.

knowledge, or a markedly one-track attitude to life, will correspondingly concentrate our interest on limited form-areas. That is how the concept we call *style* is created, style in the sense of *choice of form*.

There is, however, still one question to be asked before we go on to discuss this. Are there then no 'eternal laws' for what is beautiful, rules which will hold good in all ages? Yes, there are indeed: that is those considerations which are based on things acknowledged which we have to regard as quite fundamental and valid for all time. As might be expected, these will first and foremost be considerations based on Nature's eternal speech and influence on our minds. But the fact that these considerations are attended to, does not necessarily mean that the things appear beautiful to us. It would rather be more correct to put it the other way round and say that nothing will appear beautiful until these fundamental requirements are fulfilled.

STYLE

Even in fashioning the most utilitarian thing there is always a literally unlimited number of possible ways of doing so open to us, after the more material aspects have been taken into consideration. Between these we make a conscious or unconscious choice which in one way or another must coincide with our ideas in general. In order to discover how this choice is made, here are some exaggerated and quite imaginary examples.

First, let us imagine an unpractical and very learned mathematician who spends all day in his study and for whom Nature with its flowers and bird-song has no attraction. If we are to guess what sort of shapes such a man will like to see round him, we would say geometrical ones. That is a sphere where he is able to distinguish between figures, however complicated, and the sight of them will fill him with joy. He would build his house as a cube and give his jars and vases the shapes of parabolas and hyperbolas. He is thus a *formalist*.

In the same way we would expect a botanist to prefer shapes which are copied from Nature. He will build his house without thought of a main form, but in such a way that wood and stone are allowed to function in accordance with their original character. Branches and the stalks of flowers will be his models in constructing his furniture. He is a devotee of the *organic*.

Lastly, we can imagine an engineer, a man who has sense only for the practical and serviceable. He will be concerned with the heat-conserving properties of the walls and when it comes to deciding the shape of the roof he will choose that from which rain-water and snow will run off most easily, considering the material used to cover it. He will consider whether his coffee pot is comfortable to hold, and easy to pour from, and easy to clean. He is a (hard-boiled?) *functionalist*.

Each of these people will have made a *style* which will stamp their whole house and its furniture.

There is a good deal of truth in all that. Instead of taking individuals as our examples, we can take whole ages, and we will then see that where the people in one period were mainly concerned with mathematics, the cult of Nature or technics, they will surround themselves with corresponding shapes. We can also assume that in the form they give to things they will build on each other's experiences, they will develop and cultivate their form-language, so that their style emerges as something still more clarified and distinct. And that would still be correct, if we could look at things in bulk.

However, *such* one-sided people as these are fortunately rare. Our mathematician would presumably also like to sit in a good chair when he was working. Perhaps he would also

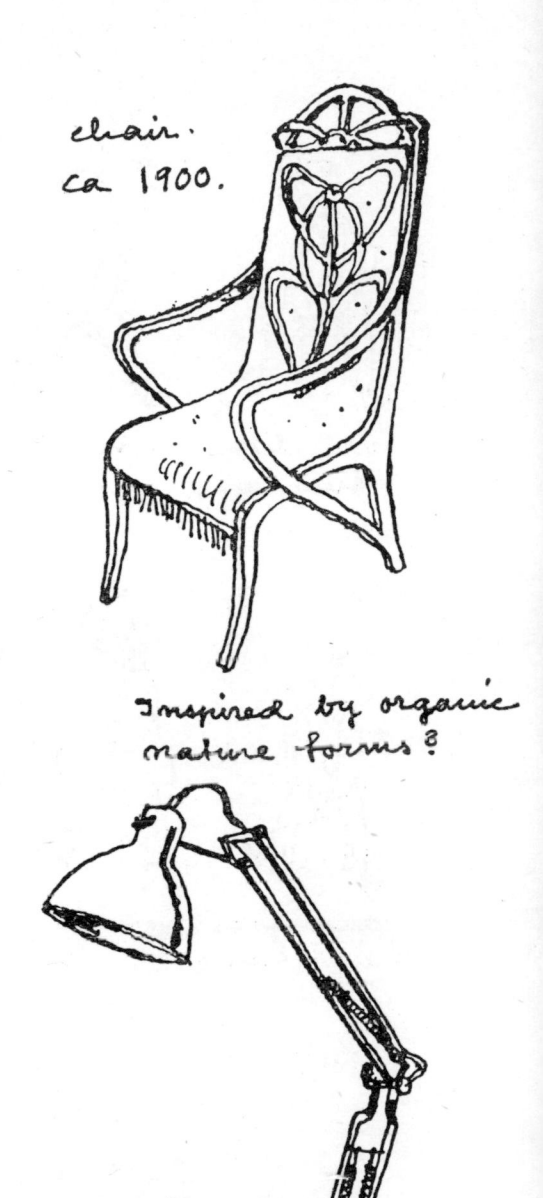

chair.
ca 1900.

Inspired by organic nature forms?

Modern draughts-man's lamp.

lucid and beautiful utility form

73

We like to be similar,

and fear what is strange.

want a change and relaxation after the day's studies and go out for a walk in the country. That, presumably, would also open his mind to the other values in the world of form and perhaps even make him wonder which gave him the greater pleasure: those which reflected his work, or those which symbolized spare time and rest.

We can now go back again to humanity as a whole and say that such antitheses will naturally have existed in all ages. And at the same time there is a multiplicity of other interests and concepts, on which we have not yet touched, each of which plays its part: religious views, amongst others. In ages of even development, however, there will be certain central integrating ideas which will stamp the picture as a whole. It is on that basis that common style is created.

We are still on a somewhat theoretical plane. In our day many attempts have been made to explain the various style-forms, but that is an impossible task. Much depends on chance; people tend to stick to the forms to which they have been accustomed, or they accept new ones (which come from outside), because they appear exciting and modern. Thus there are patterns or garments of wide local use which can be traced back to a single example which once long ago was introduced to that part of the country. Let us then proceed with all possible caution. If we do, the study of style-forms will prove useful and rewarding, and it will throw light on our own problems. Later we shall take some examples from real life and try to delve deeper into things.

WHY VIEW EVERYTHING THE SAME?

But after all, people are different, someone will say, so why cannot each follow his own ideas and surround himself with the forms he wants? Of course he may, if he will take the chance of being considered not quite right in the head.

We *want* to arrange our lives in the same way, at any rate where the main features are concerned, because that gives us a sense of security. If we are in the wilds and meet a person who appears to be more or less the same as we, both in size, facial expression and clothes, we see no reason to be afraid of him. But if we met a man with feathers in his hat, bows in his beard and an American tie, we would undoubtedly be frightened. We don't know what may not be hidden behind such trappings, though it is really no more peculiar than our own get-up.

This urge for similarity may at first sight appear somewhat degrading, so let us take comfort from the fact that it is just this which makes it possible for us to *develop* things, we being thus able to build further on each other's experiences. This is true not least in the world of form, for to create forms and shapes in which everybody can find sense and meaning is no task for the individual. A genius can suddenly break aside and show us new ways. Yet he, too, is building on other people's experience, only he sees more clearly what their complications are.

The conventional lives, as it were, in a closed room.

Once a certain idea of form, a certain way of arranging one's surroundings, has taken root, it can be difficult to destroy. Even when new conditions and ideas have made its replacement natural. When that occurs there is disagreement between people's way of living and the things that determine their existence otherwise. We then usually say that they are bound by *conventions*; that is to say: accepted forms. That state can cause distortion, which is more harmful than most people realize. You live as it were in two worlds, one real and one imaginary. There is then no longer any point in *thinking* that something is beautiful or ugly. You have to try to tidy up your ideas about things.

Our own age is rich in such antitheses, since things have

developed so quickly that not everybody is able to keep pace, or even see which changes are the important ones. Because of this we shall later in the book take our own age and examine it more closely, at any rate those features of it which affect our ideas of the form of things.

This age of ours is often called *style-less*, but we must not take that as being anything regrettable. It means that we are not so one-sided in the forms we require, that we can see the beauty both in Renaissance and Louis XVI, in the formal and in the functional. But it can also be explained by saying that we know a lot, and can experience correspondingly much. Or, again, we can say that we have become understanding, which is notoriously both a strength and a weakness.

Silver ornament, circa 1900, an artificial style, it certainly wasn't made of the right ingredients to live.

CHAPTER SIX

Which deals with the properties of the surface of things,
such as colour and texture.

THE WORLD OF COLOUR

It is difficult enough to give an account of the effects of
form, but with colour it is impossible, especially in a
book where it is not possible to demonstrate what you are
talking about, but where you have to rely entirely on words.
You can also say that this is a domain where personal
taste plays, and must be allowed to play, a decisive part.
However, some explanation of the nature of colour will
not be out of place, since colour also has an influence on our
feeling for form.

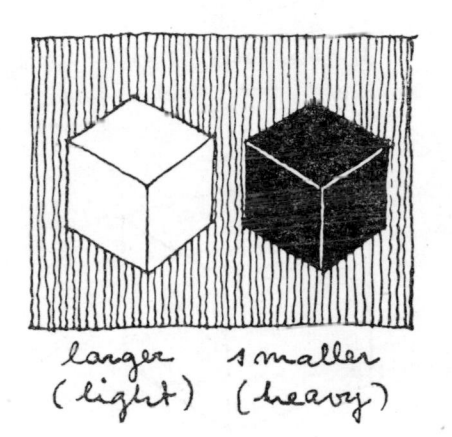

larger   smaller
(light)   (heavy)

First let us stick to black and white, and start by going
back to our cubes. The drawing in the margin shows one of
either kind. Our eye and optical nerves being adjusted as
they are, the white cube seems to be larger than the black,
though they are identical. Here we have the same effect
as that we got by putting a sharp-edged cube and one with
rounded edges alongside each other: the one which looks
largest thereby also looks the lightest. *The white cube appears*
to be lighter than the black one. Combine this with what we
learned earlier of the heavy or light effect of form, and we
will be able to achieve an even greater effect. If we paint
our heavy log cabin with tar it will appear to be even
heavier than before.

Still heavier.

Thus it is obviously right always to keep colour in mind
when we are working with forms; the best result is achieved

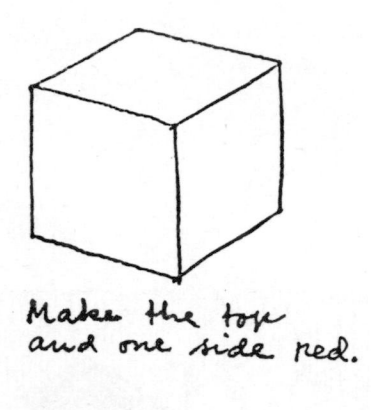

Make the top
and one side red.

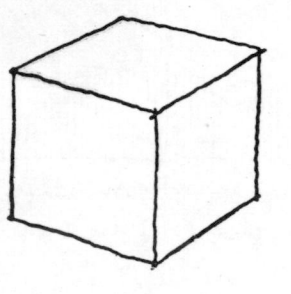

Paint the whole
cube red.

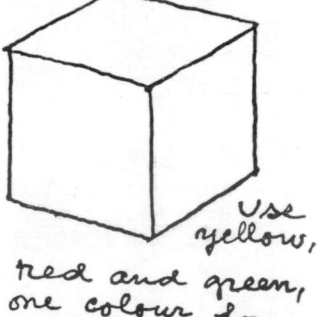

Use
yellow,
red and green,
one colour for
each side.

when the two work together. The whole then becomes clear and suited to its purpose. Conversely, you reduce the effect of existing unfortunate forms by 'painting them out', that is, by painting them with neutral colours which remove attention from them.

Take a red pencil and make two adjoining surfaces (e.g. the top and one side) of the cube in the margin red. The second side is left white. The very act of doing this will destroy something of the pure cube effect; it is as though it has ceased to be an entirely independent unit, but rather has the appearance of being a *part* cut off a greater length. The use of one colour helps to emphasize the form of a thing, while the use of several colours tends to make that form disappear.

An ordinary living-room should not give the appearance of being too enclosed, too fixed in form. If it is, we feel shut-in, get a sensation of being suffocated. Such an effect would be enhanced if we painted floor, walls and ceiling the same colour. That is why we don't do that, but usually have the walls one colour and the floor and ceiling another. It is only when the height of the ceiling is unusually great, that it will be all right to keep the same colour over-all – there will be air enough even so.

Colour the *entire* cube a fiery red and the form will again be less noticeable, simply because the strong colour catches our eye, acts as the focal point.

Now take a fresh cube and give each of its visible sides its own colour: yellow, red and green. The confusing impression becomes stronger still. Each surface acquires a life of its own: we say that the colours have *broken up* the form. At the same time we notice a new feeling of lightness, even though the colours are quite strong. This is because we have now removed all impression that the cube is made of a mass which is the same all the way through. Instead, it looks as though we were dealing with various almost separate surfaces, so thin that they can be fitted together exactly.

This is an effect we should not want our houses to have, for we like these to appear firm and solid and to make a definite form in the landscape. On the other hand, we can well imagine it being used in a room in order to get the room to appear more open and airy, which in such a case also means *larger*. In this, though, we must also take account of the various colours' own values. Some colours, the reds, appear 'close', while others, like light blue, for example, appear 'distant'. That is not just because in the latter case we think of hills showing blue in the distance or of the sky high above us. The eye's lens adjusts itself slightly differently to these colours, acting as though they really were at different distances, even when they are put side by side on one piece of paper.

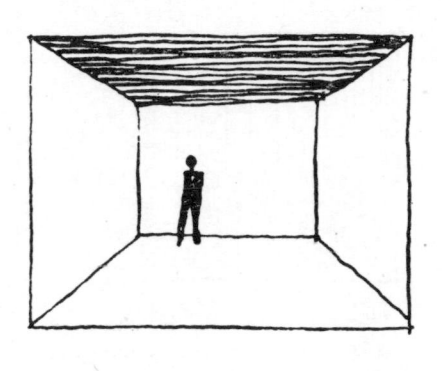

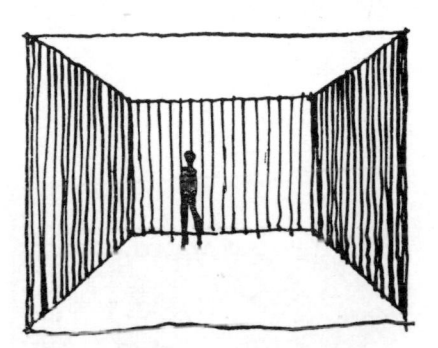

The effect of height changes with the colour of the ceiling and walls.

Lastly, we can paint a cube with splodges and stripes in all the colours we can think of and the confusion becomes complete. On the whole we can say that this has a horrific effect. In practice it is only used as a means to get shapes to disappear before our eyes. Warships and tanks are *camouflaged* in this way so as not to act as targets for the enemy. Many creatures, snakes among others, are similarly protected. When you see it spread out on a table a snake-skin can have a very marked pattern; but when on the round sinuous snake's body, where it belongs, its effect is to efface the form altogether, especially in surroundings of old leaves, grass and splodges of light and shadow.

Use different colours on the figure and the cubical form will be reduced.

Violent and diversified patterns in many colours have the same effect when used on carpets or upholstery. They give you an uncomfortable feeling, since the eye finds it an effort to keep the different forms separate.

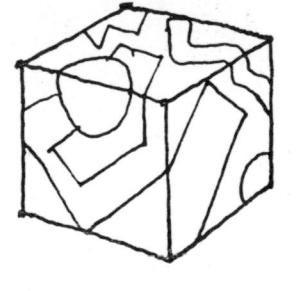

SOME GENERAL ADVICE

We all know the expression *gay* colours. It means that we consider a certain wealth of colour to be something

79

Here the different elements are clearly marked.

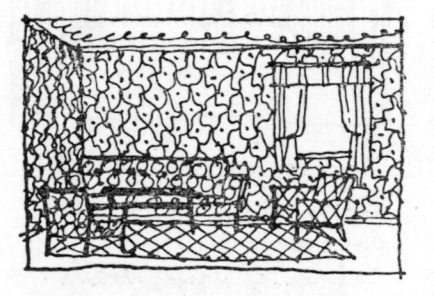

The same room. Unrestful patterns have obliterated the picture.

cheerful and pleasant, and that is a thing we ought to put into practice much more often, instead of sticking to brown, grey-brown, yellow-brown and 'beige', as so many people do. But, naturally, you have to proceed with caution in order to avoid the risks we have just mentioned. A good (though not a universal) rule is to stick to colours of the same *value*, that is to say, to colours which have approximately the same brilliancy. This is not always so easy to determine, but there is a primitive test one can make by looking at them in juxtaposition through slowly closing eyes. If the colours show a tendency to merge at a certain stage, then their values are all right. In the opposite event, the difference will be marked, right until the eyes are actually shut.

Everyone knows how to distinguish between cold colours and warm colours. Here we rely on notions from Nature: red, fire; light blue-green, ice, etc. In our climate we will as a rule prefer warm colours for the interior, for reasons which will readily be understood. But warm colours also have the effect of appearing 'closer' and the cold more 'distant', which is something we ought to remember in dealing with small, narrow rooms.

As we know, sunlight is composed of a number of colours which together form white. But two simple colours can also together form white, if they are 'complementary', as they are then called. We can also put it by saying that they keep each other in balance, an equilibrium of which the optical nerves also feel a need. Red and green in certain combinations can be such complementary colours, and as a rule it is wrong to make a red room without seeing that green is also represented in one way or another, even though it may be to a much smaller extent, as grey-green or whatever it may be. If this is not done the eye will become exhausted. But these are all very far-reaching problems, and what has been said here is only to be taken as indicating how to set about studying them for ourselves.

80

Before we leave the subject, let me just say that an interior where everything is done in shades of one and the same colour is usually considered especially choice and 'stylish'. It is the same with clothes. A woman who has hat, dress, shoes and gloves of the same colour will usually be considered very well dressed. And if, to crown it, that colour also goes with her eyes and lipstick, then she will be considered really smart. Here, however, we are not dealing only with pure concepts of beauty. We are to a large extent impressed by the fact that she has been able *to afford* to get such an outfit together. We others, whose wardrobes are more governed by chance, have to wear one of this year's garments together with others acquired the year before and the year before that. And even though their colours go excellently together the general effect is much less that of being studied. It must, though, be admitted that this use of one colour is a good way of achieving a feeling of unity and rest, and that is an important thing. Yet even with colours it is possible to establish an atmosphere of repose in tension, in the same way as is done in the world of pure form. And that makes it more significant.

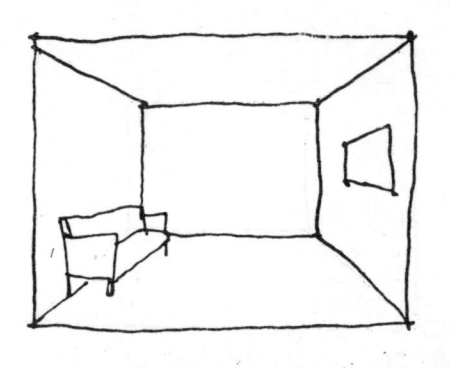

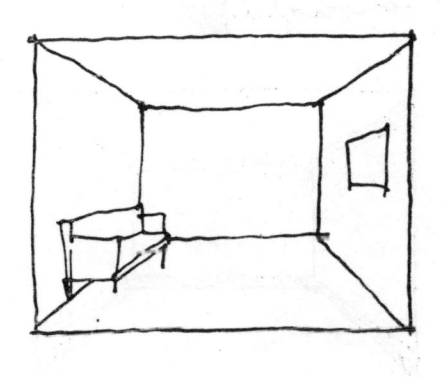

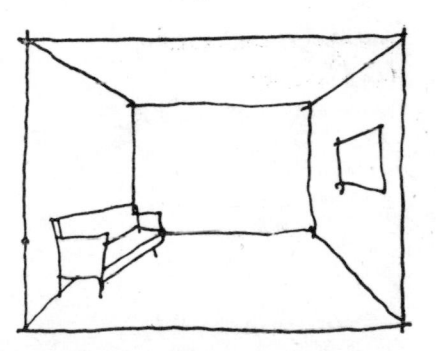

Finally, let me just mention the use we make of colour to mark structural or other important features in a building, which we may feel an urge to distinguish. We have just quoted an example, though in another connection it is true, that of painting the walls one colour and the ceiling another. Apart from the reason first given, this can serve to emphasize that wall and roof are elements of different structural character. Similarly, it would be natural to make the bearing elements in a building, such as pillars and beams, if they otherwise are a visible part of the picture. Even the colour will help to emphasize what the form has to tell.

A misconceived expression of this desire is the mania many people have for painting the roof and floor mouldings

Colour the walls and ceilings with different colours and see for yourself how the character of the room changes.

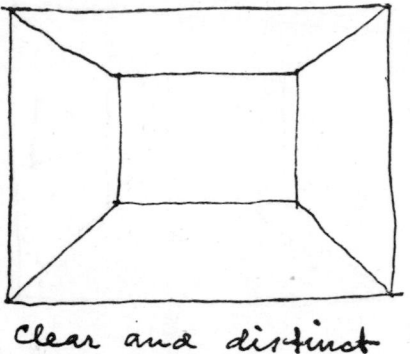

Clear and distinct enough.

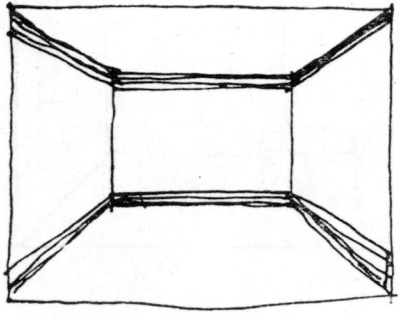

Exaggeratedly distinct

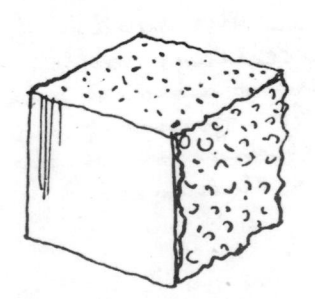

of an otherwise light room in strong colours. As we use them these mouldings are to be regarded less as important architectural features, than as trivial necessities which hide ugly transitions from one material to another. If they are marked too emphatically, the effect will be to make the top and bottom of the walls really obtrusive. This is as wearisome as when a loquacious person insists on explaining in detail things we ourselves have long since noticed.

TEXTURE AND SURFACE

Let us once again go back to the cube.

If, instead of painting the different surfaces, we try treating them with different kinds of tools, we will get a series of effects which are closely related to those we achieved with colours. If the cube is made of stone we can polish one of the sides smooth, file another rough, and score the third with a chisel. That will lead to an almost greater sense of confusion, for we get the impression that each side exhibits a fresh material without there being any connection between them. We cannot see of what stuff the cube is actually made.

Such properties of a surface as we are discussing here, we called its *texture*. Unplaned wood and sacking can be said to have roughly the same texture, despite their other differences. A smooth-planed slab of some hard wood has a texture which has quite a lot in common with tin. Similarly, cast iron can have points of resemblance with a thick closely woven woollen material. It is just as important to ensure that the different textures go together, as it is to see that colours can be combined. A thick embroidered woollen cloth does not look right on a smooth polished table-top, the difference is too great. A shiny silk cloth does not seem right either—it is too similar; you don't rightly know what is cloth and what wood. But a thin matt well-ironed linen cloth looks well, because the wood and the material bring out each other's properties in a favourable manner.

Yet it is also possible to combine strongly contrasting textures, in the same way as you can associate colours which contrast as strongly as do red and green. A delicate shiny silver buckle can be lovely on a coarse stout leather strap; but it should be observed that here we have emphasized the contrast by letting the buckle, which is so delicate, stand by itself against the big stout strap. By doing that we stressed the fact that there was also a difference in quality. The valuableness of the buckle can be set alongside the massiveness of the strap. A similar effect is to be found in the shiny brass balls they liked in the old days to put on top of heavy black cast-iron stoves. Here there is no striking difference in quality between the two materials measured in money; but emotionally it is there all the same. Also, we consider it natural for there to be an officer with sword and medals parading in front of a troop of privates, yet if there were as many officers as privates, it would no longer look so good.

It is easy and amusing to experiment with effects of texture. Small stones, bits of paper, pieces of wood and of different kinds of cloth make excellent materials. By putting them together in different ways, we will soon have our eyes opened to possibilities and values which perhaps we had not previously realized existed.

If we experiment with different textures for the treatment of walls in a room, we discover that the possibilities are the same as we had with colours. But we would be wise to be more cautious in their use. If a room is entered by a short wall, we might easily think of plastering the opposite wall smooth, while having the others rough plastered. That would make the short wall, which acts as the bottom of the room, viewed from the entrance, appear lighter or *more distant*. In one way the effect would be of still looking at

a common sin:
smooth leather
and corrugated
cloth on the same
chair. There is
no unity.

Near

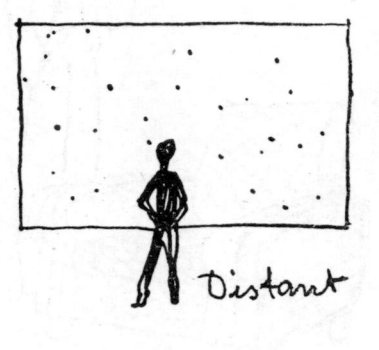

Distant

rough plaster, though at a much greater distance. But if we made the one wall of stone and had the other three papered, we would scarcely be able to be at rest in the room. It would give us a feeling of being in two houses at the same time.

Our experiments with the cube will also teach us to be cautious in treating surfaces differently on one and the same object. To do so is to deprive it of something of its true character; we do not rightly know how we are to regard it. This is exactly the same confusion as comes over us when we are confronted with a person with 'two faces'; we do not know which of them to take as the right one. None the less, this is a thing you often see done with furniture: cupboards with some polished bits and some matt; arm-chairs covered partly with corrugated cloth and partly with smooth leather. All such combinations are unpleasant, because they have a confusing effect on the form.

In the same way the use of different kinds of wood can be confusing. Some simple inlaid strips can be quite all right. If they are rightly placed, they will emphasize the main form in a good way. And there is nothing against putting many different kinds of wood together in a sort of picture (marquetry) provided the effect of flatness is retained.

It is difficult to say anything of general validity about what kind of surface treatment is to be preferred. This depends largely on the material with which we are dealing, but this all belongs to a later chapter. Having so far confined ourselves to forms like cubes and spheres, we can say that for these we prefer surfaces which are quite *precise*, and which most clearly express the fact that it is cubes or spheres we have in front of us. That is to say that they ought to have a smooth matt or semi-matt surface.

To make the surface shiny can easily prove confusing, especially where cubes are concerned. If they are glossy the different sides will mirror their surroundings, and we will see more of the reflexes from windows or lamps than we see of the surfaces themselves. Thus we can as a rule say that it is wrong to give furniture with level surfaces an entirely mirror-like surface, because the reflection will efface the impression given by the form. We are, I suppose, assuming that the form is good. On the other hand, a dull polish on the surface can bring out the light and shade and with it the form.

Things are slightly different where curved or broken forms are concerned. The light is then reflected in quite a different way, the main form being emphasized as the sketch in the margin shows. But none the less, the effect can be unfortunate in a room, because a lot of gloss and reflection makes the total effect restless and speckled. The difference between the light parts and the dark becomes too great; the eye cannot take in such great contrasts, it becomes *dazzled*.

Many homes sin in this respect. The urge to have what is shiny is probably part of the conception of what is *fine*—a way of thinking with which we will deal later.

Matt, distinct surface

Shiny, indistinct surface

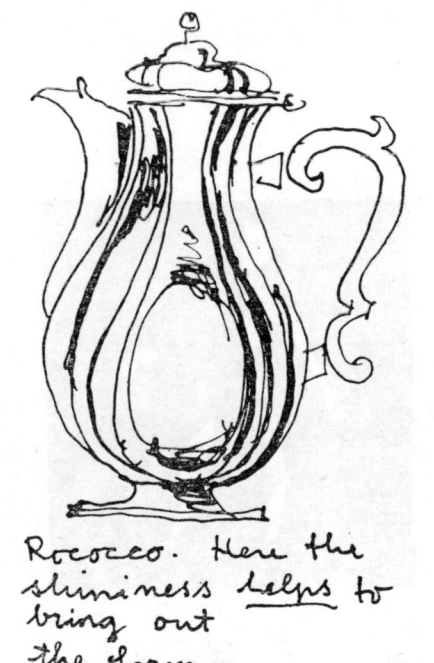

Rococo. Here the shininess helps to bring out the form.

CHAPTER SEVEN

Which tells of light and the effect it has on form.

The interpretation of good form is often a matter of collaboration between the eye and the experience of the hands. A sculptor likes to run his hands over an object which catches his attention, and we ourselves have an intuitive sense of how a surface will feel to the finger or how a thing is meant to be used. Yet in the great majority of cases it is the eye which does the more important work, and the eye is itself entirely dependent on the *light*. That is why it is important to investigate what effect light has on form.

The fact that we see an object at all is because it reflects the rays from the sun or other source of light such as an electric lamp. But the object is also lit indirectly by the rays reflected from walls, streets or other objects around it. If it was something entirely black and lustreless we should theoretically not be able to see more than the outline of it, even in the brightest sunlight. But we cannot manage to make a thing as black as that.

If we can imagine a person placed out in the ether where there are no reflexes, he would look roughly like the sketch in the margin. He is brightly illuminated on the surfaces which face the sun, but the rest of him lies in complete darkness. If he were standing on earth, the result would be not nearly so complete, since the sun's rays which were reflected from his surroundings would indirectly illuminate the bits of him in shadow. But if we put our man in a room

Man in the ether

86

which is all painted black and lit by a single lamp, we would achieve more or less the same effect as in the ether. What are we to say of this form of lighting–is it satisfactory?

No, it isn't, for it doesn't tell us everything about what we are looking at. We can, of course, assume that the man is a man, all the way round, and that the bits in shadow do not hold any particular surprises. Yet we cannot be altogether certain. If instead of a person it is something more or less unknown, the doubt will be really embarrassing. On the other hand, it must be admitted that this form of lighting has a certain *effectiveness* which is often called dramatic. It is exciting, just because certain things are lit, while others lie mysteriously in darkness. This lighting effect is often used in the theatre, especially when something unusually strange is happening. But in everyday life we have no use for it.

Now we can paint the whole room white and install a number of lamps all round it, some high, some low, and all at the same distance. If we also dress our man in white, we will discover that he, so to speak, disappears from sight, because there is no proper shadow at all. We have no means by which to register form, everything is effaced. We cannot use this way of lighting either, but then it is also very difficult to achieve.

The best form of lighting is when objects are brightly lit from one side and less brightly from the others. Form will then stand out clearly and the parts in shadow will not be so dark that we cannot see what they hold. As far as daylight is concerned, we will get the best light in a room which has a large window in one wall and a smaller window in one of the other walls. But there is no need always to stick so strictly to theory, for walls and ceiling will always reflect a lot of light, provided they are not very dark in colour.

A long room painted a dark colour which has only one window in one short wall, will undoubtedly have a bad light.

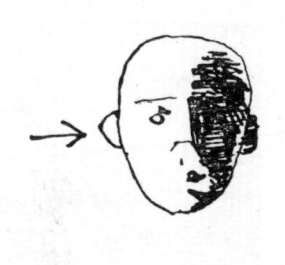

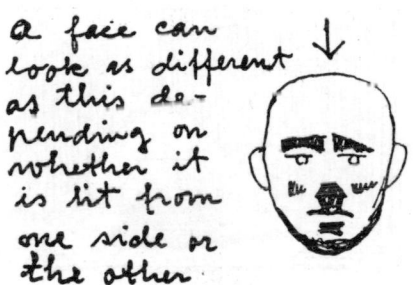

a face can look as different as this depending on whether it is lit from one side or the other

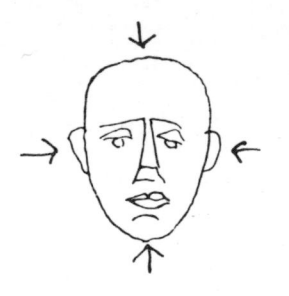

Indirect light:
a dead light.

Direct light: better.
Both lamps have
closed shades
and are not very
effective.

With a room of this shape, we ought to see that the inner short wall is painted a light colour.

Lamp-light is easier to deal with, especially electric light which enables us to have light points placed where we want them. On the whole, we can say that the same rules apply here: the best light is obtained with several sources of light, of which one can be dominant. It goes without saying that you place the lamps where you have most need for them: on the work-table, where you are reading, etc.

You should always avoid placing powerful lights close up against a wall or the ceiling. If you do that it is easy to get unpleasant shadows thrown round them and the impression of unity will be destroyed by the presence of brightly illuminated patches and ones in deepish shadow on the same surface.

DAZZLE

The greatest difficulty in the lighting of rooms is the phenomenon known as *dazzle*. This is a thing which happens when we look at a strongly concentrated light surface. We can then see nothing of what is round about it. The eye receives a shock, which destroys the ability to see for a shorter or longer period. Inside a room even the brightest daylight does not give rise to any dazzle problems as long as the window, which lets it in, is of a reasonable size. This is because the light is distributed over such a large surface. But even so, the contrast between the window area and the shaded wall in its immediate vicinity can be so great as to seem unpleasant. For that reason not even the window wall ought to be too dark. A simple and well-known means of mitigating the abrupt transition, which we all use, is to hang up curtains on either side. If the curtains are of thick opaque material they serve no purpose, for they merely reduce the light opening and make the room darker. But if they are translucent, the light will be broken up and spread by them. The light in the room will become softer and all dazzle will disappear.

Dazzle is much more difficult to deal with when it is caused by electric light, where all the light is concentrated in a tiny spiral wire in the bulb. What has to be done here is to get the light distributed over a sufficiently large surface, so that the light per surface unit is no stronger than the eye can support. The simplest method is to hang a globe of matt or cloudy glass round the bulb, so that the light is caught by the glass and you get the impression that it is the globe itself which is shining. Some of the brilliancy is lost, it is true, by doing that, but not so much.

It is important to remember that dazzle is not directly dependent on the power of the lamp. What is decisive is its relation to its surroundings. Of course, there are lights so strong that under no circumstances can the eye bear to look straight at them; as is the case with the sun. But we can be completely dazzled by staring into the bulb of a pocket torch in dark surroundings, while in daylight we would scarcely be able to see that it was even turned on. Similarly, a lamp seen against a wall or ceiling painted a dark colour is more dazzling than one which has a light background. This effect is all the greater as a lamp with dark surroundings has to be more powerful, since the dark colour reflects less of its light. This is another reason for using light colours in ordinary interiors.

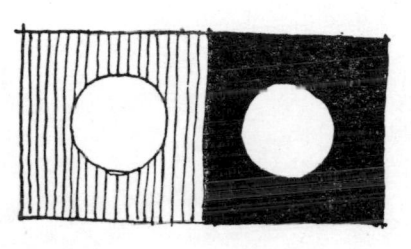

White is more dazzling on the black background.

But to colour the globe some dark translucent colour serves no purpose other than to shut in a lot of the light. You might just as well put in a weaker bulb. On the other hand, you get a different colour in the light that does come through.

If we surround the bulb with a closed metal funnel the dazzle will, of course, vanish altogether, but then the light will have very little possibility of being spread about the

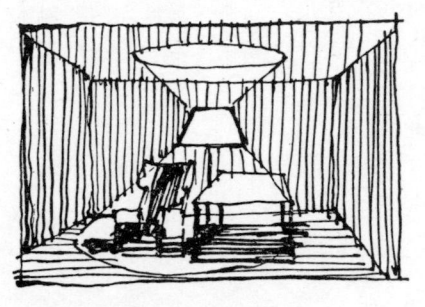

a shade which gives a good effect and all round lighting.

room. It can only flow out through the wide end of the funnel; but from there it issues all the more concentrated, especially if the inside of the funnel is made white or shiny like a mirror. If the funnel has the correct shape the light which strikes the sides will be reflected out through the opening. We use such lamps when we want to have a limited area strongly illuminated, like a drawing-board or a reading-desk. But such light gives strong shadows.

If we twist such a lamp round to face the ceiling, the room will be lit by the rays reflected from the surface of the ceiling. The lighter the colour of this surface, the better the light in the room. This method of lighting is called *indirect*, because we do not use the rays coming directly from the source of the light, but only those which are reflected. But the rays off a matt surface will go in all directions and give blurred shadows. We often say of it that it is a 'dead' light. It is also uneconomical, for much of the light is absorbed by the ceiling, even if that is white. Combined with points of more 'live', shadow-throwing light, however, it can make a serviceable form of general lighting for a room.

The lamp-shades now most generally used and in many respects the best it is possible to have, are slightly funnel-shaped, open top and bottom, with lateral surfaces made of light, refractive material. In this way, the bulb itself is screened at all levels in which the eye is normally likely to be, while the light can stream unhindered downwards towards your book or knitting, and upwards to cause reflexes from the ceiling. Thus such a lamp acts simultaneously in all the ways we have so far mentioned.

If such a lamp is placed on a table, the top of the table ought also to be light in colour or perhaps be covered with a white cloth so that the light thrown down is also reflected. This is not just to make the most economical use of the current being consumed, but because it makes the lighting of the room richer, more alive. In the old days of the paraffin lamp, when artificial light was a more costly thing than it is now, people paid attention to such matters and it was usual to spread a white 'light cloth' on the table under the hanging lamp.

As you can see, the problem of the light is the most important of all when we are dealing with rooms and forms, whether the light be artificial or daylight. On proper lighting, too, depends our efficiency at work. It is thus strange that there is scarcely any sphere in which people exhibit less understanding. Lamps are placed just any-where without thought of where the light ought to fall, and they are covered with shades which may well be 'amusing' or 'cosy', but which in actual fact steal most of the light. In the great majority of homes there is far too little light. It is considered to be more snug and pleasant like that, but in the long run it is just tiring both to the eyes and to the mind. Look how many people always wear glasses these days. Let us try and see if we cannot avoid that fate, if there is still time. It is just a question of giving a thing thought, instead of *thinking* it to be this or that.

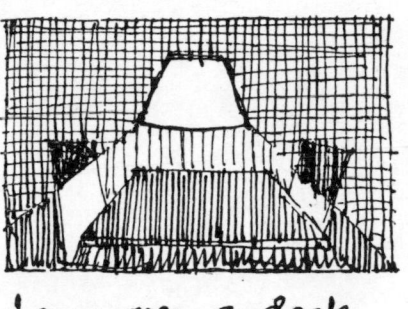

Lamp over a dark table-top.

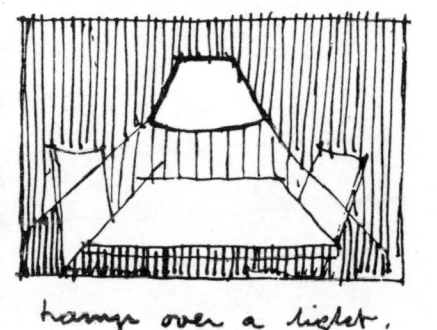

Lamp over a light table-top.

Greater effect, richer light.

CHAPTER EIGHT

In which at last we consider things jointly and against the historical background.

Let us now see if we cannot assemble the observations we have made and the views stated and use them to get a picture of the whole.

It might be best first to take some examples of the forms and interiors of previous ages and see if what we have discovered will also apply to what we find there. Antiquity is more easy to observe, since we see it at a distance and so we are not so easily confused by the many unessential details. We are better able to take in the whole, apprehend what is the main thing in the situation. But it is obvious that there will also be a danger of our over-simplifying, and we must be prepared for that. In a book like this we are forced to simplify consciously in order to reduce the problems to manageable proportions. That has to be stressed lest, after reading this, anyone should imagine that he knows all about the milieus and things we are going to describe. Anyway, the purpose of this exposition is not so much to state a number of hard and fast facts, but to set our powers of observation and thought going.

THE FARM-HOUSE ROOM

The first of our examples is an old farm-house and the one chosen is the famous Løkrestuen at Maihauga, in Norway, which can be taken as a good example, particularly

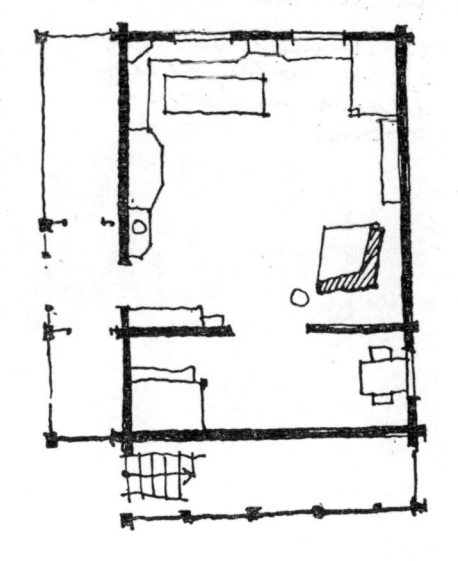

Lökrestuen —
norwegian farm house.

where furniture is concerned. Almost all farm-houses in the Norwegian valleys were built like this one, right from the time people learned to make brick fireplaces and chimneys until the 1800s.

This is itself an important point to notice. It indicates an even assured state of affairs, in which it was possible for habits and forms to crystallize, which is exactly what we find. Because of that most authorities agree that it is also a fine example of the art of furnishing and of sound sense of form. It is true that its plan and its furniture do not seem so wonderful to us; nor would we ever think of copying it, but we can learn a lot from the fine connection between form, ideas and way of life which it expresses.

The ground plan is entirely dominated by the big living-room, and it is in that that we shall spend most of our time.

Peasant ornamentation
is violent, both in
form and colours.

It should be seen
along with heavy
beams in dark
rooms.

When we enter it, we have the great fireplace facing us, and away in the other corner on the same wall is a bed. Beside the fireplace stands a chopping-block.

On the left of the entrance door stands a small bench and on it a mixing tub filled with whey for all who are thirsty. Then comes the big cupboard, beyond it a long seat running all round the wall to the bed in the other corner and only broken by the clock between the two windows. In the angle of the long seat is a small corner-cupboard. Both benches, seat and cupboards are *fixed to the wall*. Then comes the great long table which is placed by the seat, and that's all. Apart from the actual fireplace everything is made of deal of powerful dimensions, from the round logs of the walls to the stout boards of the long table.

Therein lies the first pleasant impression: a feeling of organic cohesion which has its origins in uniformity of material and the dimensions which suit it. The spacious dimensions, about nineteen feet by twenty-three feet, and the open furnishing give a good sense of repose and permanence.

The furniture is really very simple. Only the cupboards have any richness of form, with stout panels and strong colours. In a modern room they would be overpowering, but in these surroundings they seem to belong. The sparse light mitigates the violent effect.

How did the room come to be made thus, and how was it used? Before answering this, we must first see what sort of people lived in it and what they did.

Their lives were fearfully simple compared with ours. For one thing, the children had no prep. to do in the evenings—all learning was done at school during the short period which that lasted. There was none of father having to sit quiet at the desk, and as far as noise from the children was concerned, they were kept in bounds by very different methods from those we try to practise. There were no books,

94

except perhaps a Bible and Psalm Book, and no wireless. There was hard work both indoors and out, but not of the nerve-racking kind which much of ours is. For that reason relaxation was an unknown idea, and rest meant the same as sleep. To be able to 'be by oneself' is important for people who are overburdened with repressions, but you could not say that of those people. If they wanted to cry, their answer was to go outside behind the barn, and they took their love troubles to the paddock, or to the cows in the byre.

There was peace and quiet and order in things. Sedate deliberate talk, hard and fast rules for how to behave in various situations. But the most permanent thing of all was the relationship between the family, the house and the ground they owned. It was an unshakeable unit, and the man of the house, one of a line, was the hub round which everything turned.

It is this permanence which is directly evident in the furniture which is correspondingly permanent, even fixed to the walls. And the people even had their permanent places at table according to rank and dignity, the master of the house being seated on the bench at the end of the table, in the *high seat*. The arrangement of everything in the room is based on this permanence and their experience of what was the most serviceable. And what was serviceable was the same in all homes. Another technical point we can see put into practice here is the arrangement of the seats diagonally facing the hearth, where they would get most benefit from the warmth.

The requirements of the housewife do not seem to have been catered for. However, the food was simple, and the rough work, the actual cooking, was done outside in the kitchen shed.

Here we have a markedly *functional* arrangement of the room which has been welded into a permanent and

Cupboard with Renaissance motives (Normandy). Styles have a different ring to them in the unchanging peasant milieu.

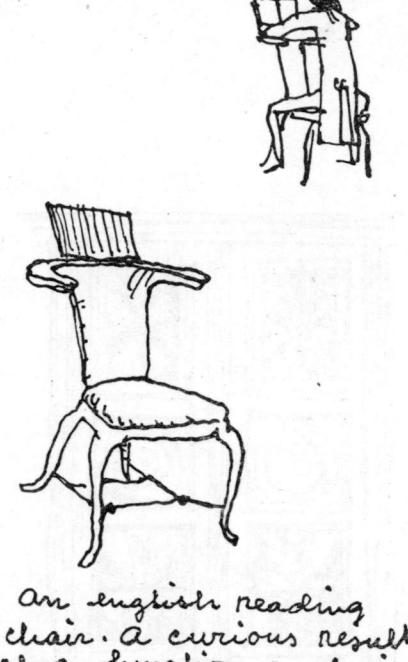

an english reading chair. a curious result of a function analysis in the 1700's.

characteristic form that is itself easy to grasp. We understand so well what it has to tell us. We can also call the furnishing and arrangement of the room *organic*, not just because of the effect of the materials, which we have already mentioned, but because the things have, as it were, grown together into an indivisible unit. *Wealth*, the surplus, has found expression in the cupboards which also contain the family's valuables, the goblets and silver spoons and other fine things which were produced on special occasions, when, too, the walls were decorated with rugs. This ability to use the room's equipment to distinguish between everyday and special occasions is another thing to note. We put out all our flags, and so we have grown afraid of days like Christmas and birthdays, for we have nothing tucked away or saved which we can bring out for such occasions.

There is not a great deal to be said about the other rooms in Løkrestuen. Off the big room is a *closet* with a fixed bed. If there were hired hands on the farm they usually slept in there, while the young owner and his wife slept in the big room. Many farm-houses had no more rooms than these, but this house also has another room above the closet. Here there is only a bed, but the room could not be used in winter as it has no means of heating. In the winter they all must have fitted into the big room as best they could.

INVENTIONS AND IMPROVEMENTS

We know that the room we have just described was an improved and further developed form of the primitive room which had a hearth in the middle of the floor and no other light than that which came through the smoke-hole in the roof. The chimney and the introduction of window-glass have provided new possibilities.

The farmer, of course, had not discovered glass—that was imported from outside, but on the whole we must be careful to avoid thinking that new forms of heating, new types of furniture, and that sort of thing, suddenly came about because someone had made a new 'invention'. Rather we should take it that the new things had come about of necessity as a result of new needs coinciding with greater economic powers and increased efficiency in handicrafts. Handicraft *methods* and materials on the whole remained the same from the Middle Ages up to the Machine Age.

The form of heating always determines the form both of the house and of the fitting-up of the individual room. The greatest event here was the transition from the open hearth to fireplace with chimney, and from the latter to the stove of cast iron. The first stoves in Norway were made at the end of the seventeenth century, and there was no further change until the introduction of central heating and electrical heating in our own century. Nowadays we can place the heating elements wherever we wish in a room, and the rooms themselves can be grouped without having to consider whether they abut on a chimney.

Lighting is also important. The open hearth and the fireplace also acted as sources of light along with tallow candles. But that light was pretty meagre, and in those days people were more dependent on daylight for working than we are, and there was no real improvement until about a hundred years ago when the paraffin lamp was invented. This stood on the table or hung over it from the ceiling, with the family gathered round. Now we have electric light which allows us to perform any kind of work all round the clock if we so wish, and which enables us to have our light-points placed just where we most need them.

Certain 'inventions' have also been made in furniture. The oldest types of furniture were the table, the bench, the bed and the chest. They were preferably made of whole planks, so that, for example, the breadth of a table depended on how broad a plank it was possible to obtain.

Stove, like a temple. 1800. Norway.

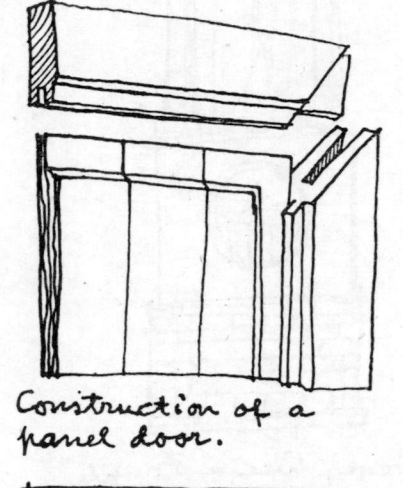

Construction of a
panel door.

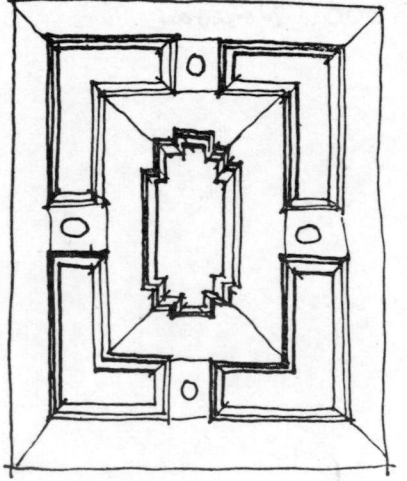

Cupboard door with
panelling. Renaissance.
Clear connection between
form and technique.

Gradually, as people acquired more and more things to look after, they began to need cupboards and these became general in the sixteenth century. A cupboard, however, was cumbersome when it had to be made of whole planks which also were very apt to crack; so carpenters learned to make sides and doors of *frames* and *panels*, as in the sketch in the margin. This form of construction also adds considerably to the appearance of an article, and we soon find cabinet-makers delighting in making frames in a great variety of ways and giving them fine profiles at the edges. The cupboard became a symbol of prosperity; it became the chief piece of furniture and people liked it to be large and to look bulky.

Chairs as such first became usual at that time, at any rate in the towns, for reasons which we shall discuss in another connection. The early ones were pretty rigid and hard to sit on, but the demand for comfort soon made itself felt and by the beginning of the eighteenth century we find individual chairs which provide all we could require in that direction. But it is not everybody who *wants* comfort. A hundred years later, during the period of Empire, they made chairs which were purposely uncomfortable. And even though they did have backs, it was not considered manners to lean back on them.

Along with chairs came the need for small tables which could be placed near them, and for card-tables.

A little later came furniture with *drawers*, the chest of drawers with big drawers and the bureau with a flap for writing, and small drawers. People had more small things to be kept, and writing had now become more general, whether it was the writing of letters or the keeping of accounts. Because of that there was more paper for which a place had to be found, and cabinet-makers had to rise to the occasion and satisfy those new requirements. All sorts of handles and bindings were now made of brass, for rough wrought-iron did not go so well on such pieces.

Larger musical instruments, like the spinet, were also a feature of the eighteenth century. Later their place was taken by the piano.

Essentially, that completes the list of the most important elements in the furnishings of our homes such as we conceive them. The things with which *we* surround ourselves, all belong to one or other of those groups. Nor have we added so very much to the selection of materials we use. We have steel and the plastics with which we are busy experimenting. One of the most important innovations is our treatment of wood by glueing together thin sheets placed criss-cross and then fixing a thin veneer on top. That enables us to have whole slabs of wood of large dimensions without their warping or needing to be especially thick.

Now we can go back to another interior of the olden days.

The bureau and the comfortable chair were inventions of the 18th century

A BURGHER'S HOME IN THE SEVENTEENTH CENTURY

On page 101 is a picture of a home which belongs to the same cultural epoch as the Løkrestuen farm-house, but which is *urban*. It would have been good if we could have used an example which still exists so that we could have gone and studied it afterwards, but very few now remain, at any rate, in my country.

The reason for this is easy to see: in a town things *change* much more. Old houses have to give place to new, and even when they remain standing new people move in and out. Urban society is more restless, and people do not have the same sense of permanence as they do in the country. The townsman consequently makes his furniture movable, he has loose individual pieces.

There is another point: those who live in the towns have many different occupations: one is a merchant, another an artisan, and another a schoolteacher. The work done in the

Renaissance cupboards
were often made with
pillars and cornices —
like a house.

home and the way people live in it are not the same in all houses, though the urge to have things similar is still there. A functional arrangement and equipment is no longer good enough–something different has to be found, something more neutral.

Let us examine a Dutch interior from the middle of the seventeenth century as it was painted by Cornelius de Man. It depicts an ordinary burgher's home, which has just received a visit from an itinerant artisan. In the margin, too, is a sketch-plan of the room. This is partly based on guess-work, for the painting only shows a section of the room, but the lighting in the picture and our knowledge of what was usual in those days make it reasonably certain to be correct.

We can see at once that not only the furnishings and arrangement, but also the whole atmosphere, is fundamentally different from the farm-house. The room is dominated by a fireplace and chimney which stands in the *middle* of one long wall, and in front of it is a table standing by itself roughly in the *middle* of the floor. Opposite the fireplace is a chest in the *middle* of the opposite long wall (in the picture it has been pulled a little way out into the room). In the external short wall are two windows, set at equal distances from the two corners, and on the wall facing them stands a large cupboard, again in the *middle*. Apart from these, there are only a few chairs which are also placed regularly.

The walls of the room are of brick with grey-white plaster. The fireplace has (possibly) columns of polished stone standing against a background of glazed ceramic-tiles. The floor, too, is flagged in a pattern of squares which emphasizes the regularity of the room's arrangement. The cornice of the fireplace, the big cupboard and the beams in the ceiling are of dark, finely worked oak.

This, too, must be called a beautiful room. Its fittings

100

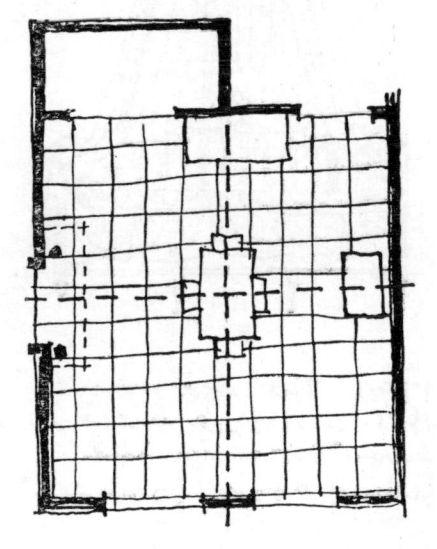

a renaissance interior.

have forms which are clean and distinct, easy to apprehend, and you get a feeling of square-set permanence both from the individual pieces of furniture and from the way they are set together. The architecture of the fireplace and cupboard is mainly a matter of horizontal and vertical effects, and the detail is on the same scale. The heavy curtains in deep colour of the four-poster bed make a contrast which adds a necessary touch of snugness.

What strikes us most is the strictly symmetrical treatment of the room. We can draw straight lines through fireplace–table–chest, and through cupboard–table–centre between windows, which are *axes* binding the whole together with great force. Here it is no longer the *functional*, but the *formal*, ideals which have determined the room's arrangement.

We have already partly explained why this is; but if we are to appreciate properly what we see, it must be added

101

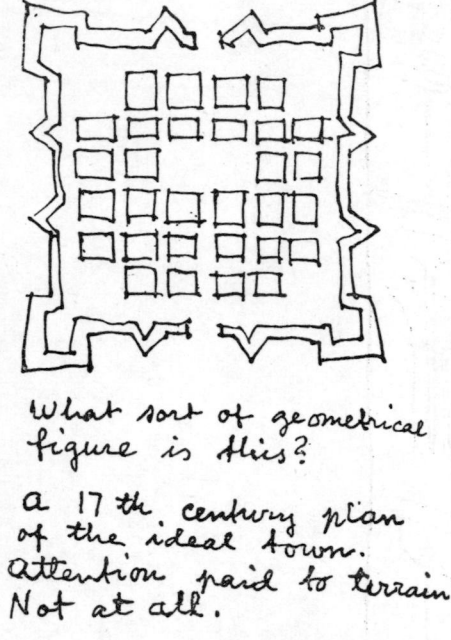

What sort of geometrical figure is this?

a 17th. century plan of the ideal town. attention paid to terrain? Not at all.

1790. The bed was still a usual piece of furniture in the living room (Sweden)

that the people who laid the basis for this room-shape were greatly occupied with their importance as human beings. They wanted to rule Nature, not subordinate themselves to it. They were very keen on *order* as an emanation of thought, of mental activity. And theirs was an age which produced a number of great thinkers, men who laid the foundations of modern mathematics and other exact sciences. In all modesty the room tells us much of all this.

Most of *us* would call such a room stiff and boring, and it is correct that it does not bear the stamp of any special activity or variety of activities. But just because of that it could be used for a little of everything. And so it had to be, for it was there that the family spent their time, day and night. In it they worked, had their meals and slept. At night the entire family, or most of them, huddled together in the bed in the corner. The smallest first, of course, which is why there was that thick curtain, to make the bed more or less dark and peaceful inside. And snug; we must not forget that, for those rooms were usually cold and draughty.

Life in the town was not very much more complex than in the country. Peace in one's private life had not then become a thing people *had* to have. The only indication that people had begun to distinguish between domestic activities, is that the *kitchen* has now been moved out into its own room which has a large fireplace, and to which, as well as the preparation of food, other such domestic activities as spinning, cobbling, etc., were relegated. The living-room had become more of a reception-room.

DESIGN BASED ON USE

In these two examples we have confined ourselves almost entirely to the arrangement and equipment of the living-room. In farm-houses such as that shown on page 93 there were scarcely any other rooms, but town houses were often large and multifarious. However, the other rooms, and even the design, are of little interest to us in this connection, for they were not used directly by the family, were not part of a whole, as rooms in our houses are. We prefer to have rooms for different kinds of purpose, but that is a relatively new idea. In olden days people looked at things differently and that by no means for reasons of economy. Even Charles XV, who lived at the end of last century and had space enough at his disposal, had his bedroom so arranged that he could have his meals, work and receive visitors in it. Such an arrangement hardly conforms with our notion of the princely.

But even after it became general, at any rate among the well-to-do, for people to use several rooms, the ground-plans do not tell us very much about *what* the rooms were used for. Reproduced here is the plan of Damsgård, a big house in Bergen which received its final form during the eighteenth century. It has big rooms and small rooms, but, like the furniture in the burgher's room we have just been considering, these are arranged symmetrically, that is, according to a pattern, not with any view to their use. There are few corridors, so that to get to the inner rooms you have to go through the others.

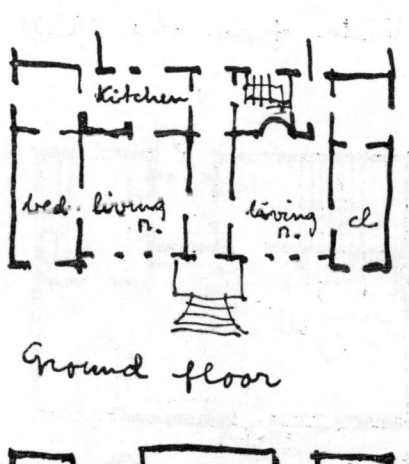

We, who think that children should be able to go to the bathroom at night and that their night's rest should not be disturbed because there happen to be guests in the house, consider this a thoroughly impractical arrangement. Also, we think that a dining-room ought to be of a different shape and smaller than a living-room, which latter ought to have large windows for the sake of the view. But obviously those who built Damsgård thought otherwise. That was not because they had not come so far in their understanding of things as we, but because they had other needs. To them it was more important to have a pleasant sense of formal order, with dimensions and units recurring throughout the

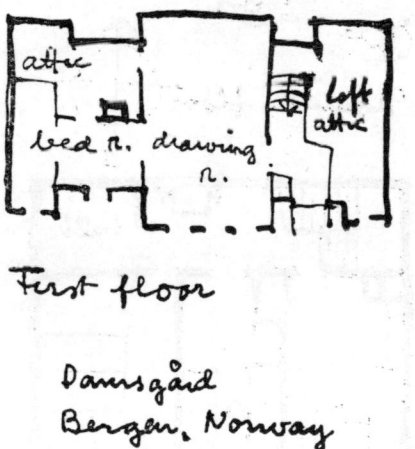

Damsgård
Bergen, Norway

Villa from the 1930's.

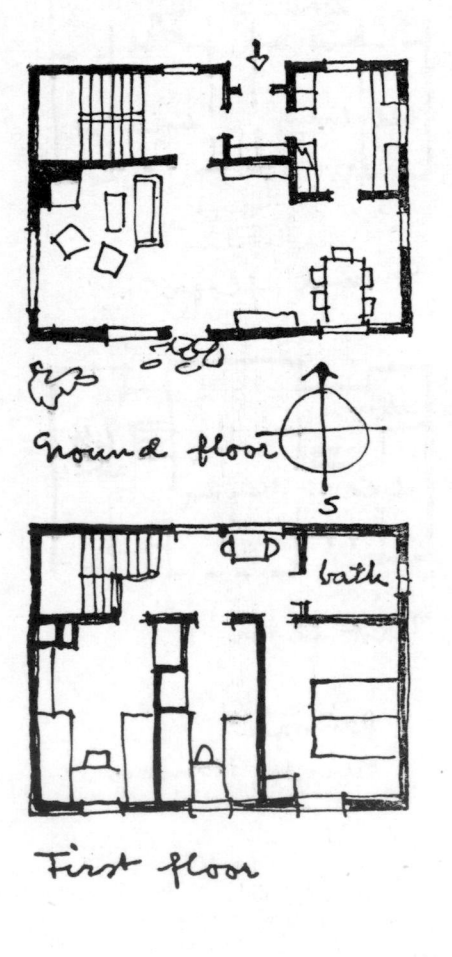

Ground floor

bath

First floor

house. People of slender means in thickly populated areas had to content themselves with rooms which were stamped by the need to economize and by the needs of daily life; but if you had money and power you ought also to emphasize the fact that you were *not* affected by material considerations. By granting all the requirements of the formal you elevated your life to a higher level. That is more or less what they must have thought.

New conditions of work, new forms of experience and ways of living have changed all that. We shall not explain the whole process here, but merely point out that a decisive factor was the great new demand for hygiene, both physical and mental. This resulted in designs which attempted to cater for those requirements so that all might have them and not only the well-to-do. Even where pecuniary considerations restricted the space available, everything had to be arranged in the best way. After that, however, it was no use clinging to ideals of a formal nature. They required too much space. Therefore we now make a virtue of necessity, and cultivate the beauty in the *utilitarian*, and hope that we will also be able to get the whole to appear *organic*.

For comparison with the mansion at Bergen, here is a typical plan for a small villa from the 1930s. In this symmetry has gone by the board. The next thing to notice is its orientation in relation to the sun. This was something quite new. The kitchen faces east, so that it enjoys the morning sun but escapes the great heat later in the day. The dining space has a window facing south, so that it gets the greatest possible amount of sunshine, while the living-room has a large window to the west. It is mostly in the afternoon and evening that this is used, and the house should preferably be sited so that there is an opportunity to enjoy the view from it; which can also be done from the terrace outside.

The three bedrooms are by themselves on the first floor,

and there is direct access to each from the passage, so that no one disturbs anyone else. There are two rooms for the children (boys and girls) and one for the parents. Then there is a bathroom, and this also faces east, so that the morning sunshine can provide a little encouragement before the day's work begins. The size of all rooms is carefully adjusted to the purpose they are to serve, strict regard being paid to economy.

The things just mentioned are but a small part of the multitude which an architect of today tries to remember when he is planning such a house; but they give a good picture of how complicated our problems have become, how many practical points we have to try to take into consideration. And even so, we have forgotten one of the most important: that the house should be easy to run. For we think that we have so many tasks of equal interest that neither housewives nor others have any time to waste.

And now we can well ask: *Has* our new house become organic? Has it acquired that cohesion in forms and dimensions which we require if we are to be able to live in it, or has it become an agglomeration of problems, solved well enough individually, but not as a whole? It will not be easy to give an answer until the process of development has been better explained. But much would seem to indicate that we shall have to try to simplify it one way or another, try to assemble our divided interest which at the moment embraces so much from the past and the future which is beyond its range. Then perhaps our design will settle down a bit more. The same goes for fittings and furniture, a subject to which we shall now revert.

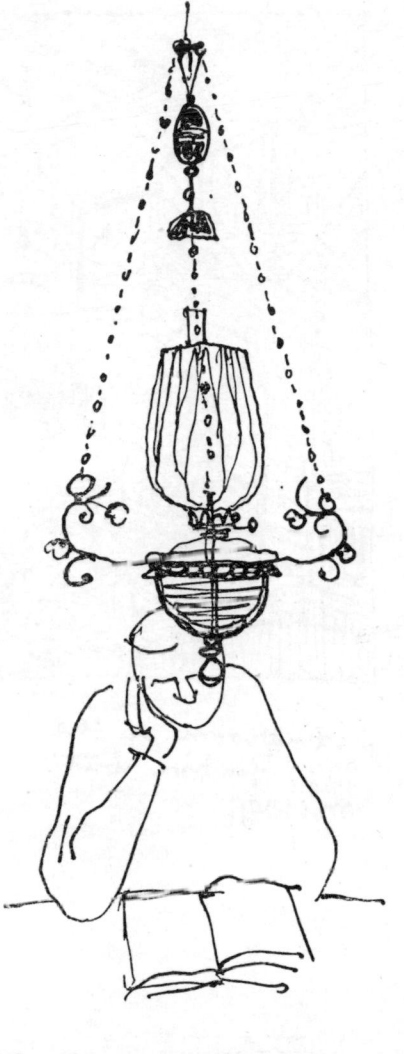

Typical picture of the cultured 80's: Reading under an elegant paraffin lamp.

THE 'EIGHTIES

Here is a sample from an ordinary middle-class home in the days when the sitting-room really began to become a

Sittingroom of the '80's, festive but messy

sitting room as we understand it, with special rooms allotted to sleeping, cooking and other special activities. We have chosen the period around 1880.

There is no end to the furniture here. In one corner is a piano set aslant, in the other stands a large well-upholstered sofa. Then there is a small table (which the eighteenth century introduced along with coffee, tea and chocolate drinking); then a bureau. Then come chairs of various kinds. The most comfortable are assembled in the corner round the sofa, under the hanging lamp. This is already quite a lot, yet the room is filled with a further multitude of *things*. Things which only the rich used to have, had by now become so very much cheaper (and worse) thanks to the assistance of the machine, that it was no wonder that people wanted to take advantage of the fact and get themselves some of this and that.

Besides all this there are some peacock's feathers and conch-shells which Uncle Henry, the sea captain, brought home. Then some pressed flowers in glass frames from the place to which father and mother went on their honeymoon. And *photographs* of relatives and friends. (That was another innovation.) But they provide pleasant *memories* in a way that is both festive and stimulating, and the children enjoy looking at them and hearing about it all. Yet as though that were not enough, there are tassels on the lamps, pompons on table-cloths and chairs, and large plants in the corners. There are tall doors taken from an Italian palace and a wonderful panelled ceiling, their idea of what people used to have in medieval castles. Those, too, are romantic reminders.

Villa or romanesque cathedral?
Oslo, 1860.

All this is amusing in its way, festive and luxurious, and luxury is certainly a thing to hold on to. But it also gives a picture of a violent clash between old concepts on the one side and new possibilities and new requirements on the other. In this clash *form* has gone by the board, and there has resulted a formless chaos: among all this welter there is nothing on which the eye can rest, no main feature to hold on to, even though symmetry remains the guiding principle.

We are perhaps inclined to smile a little at all the historical reminders, but in the name of truth it should be pointed out that the mid-nineteenth century was just the time when historical research began as a new and exact science. People *knew* more about the past, and we have often explained that sense for form is connected with what we know. And it is when our knowledge is quite new that we are most concerned with applying it. In the same way our age has cultivated the streamlined form in season and out, for we are so proud of having grasped it.

We must admit that our interiors have gained a lot in sense of harmonious restfulness, spaciousness and order.

OUR OWN ROOM

Here we have furnished the living-room from the villa in the previous example. Not as everyone would have done, but roughly as we must assume the architect would have intended it. The furniture is shown in the sketch and there is no need to enumerate what the various things are and what they are used for. We are familiar with them all.

What we should notice is that as far as the different articles and groups of furniture are concerned the arrangement is no different in essentials from that of the 'eighties. Our requirement that the room should be capable of a variety of uses was already formulated in those days. In a corner by itself we see the fireplace, then there is the sitting-group, the work-place and a few trivialities in between. Perhaps we have done this or that to make individual articles a little more serviceable for their various purposes.

108

But to get order and totality in this multiplicity, we have *organized* it all in a clearer way, assembled the groups in more characteristic units, moved them up to the walls to gain space, so that the floor has become free again. We have removed the prisms and pompons, not only to make it easier to keep clean (although that also plays a part), but to get the forms more distinct. We want to know what it is we are looking at.

It may be that this room is as good as we could wish, or as we can manage to get it. Much points to that being so. But we must not regard it as a formula for what is correct, for our requirements can change quickly. The important thing is to consider whether things are arranged and formed in keeping with ourselves, our own situation, both as individuals and as members of a community. Therefore we had best discuss this situation a little.

CHAPTER NINE

Which deals with subversive elements, like reproductions and fakes.

Silver coffee pot from the 1880's. Oslo.

Supposed to remind the norwegians that they are descended from vikings, and so make them correspondingly resolute.

While describing the interior of the 'eighties in the previous chapter we made acquaintance with one or two notions which we had not previously discussed. We discovered that there were certain things put there as reminders and that many of the things in the room were cheap machine-made products of doubtful worth. That again reminds us of the opposite concept: that of quality.

Before discussing our own position let us go into these notions a little, for they play a large part in our lives today.

THE REMINDER

Here, for a change, is a little tale.

Once upon a time there was a king of the Negroes. He was a mighty man who had power of life and death over his subjects. Ruling others was the nicest thing he could think of.

There was only one thing which the king feared and that was the lions which roamed the forests round about and killed people and cattle. Then he hit upon the idea of having a throne made which reminded him of a lion. Once he had plucked up courage to sit on it, when he had got his heavy body actually planted on the back of the wooden lion, he was able to tell himself that he wasn't afraid of lions any longer, since he ruled over them too.

And his subjects let themselves be taken in by this and became even more frightened of the cruel king than they had been before.

Then some people got together and came to the conclusion that it was wrong to have such a despotic king. There ought not to be a king at all—the power in the land ought to be wielded by a council of men elected by the people. They explained this to everybody and the people thought it made sense. But they were afraid of the king who sat on the lion. Then someone reminded them that the lion was made of wood and wasn't in the least dangerous. It was just a *symbol*. And so they killed the king.

The people then had the power, which was right and proper as things were then. But they, nevertheless, lacked a sign that would show that now it was their turn to govern, and so they also made themselves wooden lions to sit on. They did this not so much because the wooden lions reminded them of real lions, but because they reminded them of the old king.

This was a thing they should not have done, for because of it they all came gradually to acquire the habits and way of thinking of the old king.

That is just a tale, but it accords quite well with the truth. This business of taking symbols from Nature has been done countless times and in countless ways, from lions as thrones to young girls' rooms papered with a design of bluebells. There is nothing to be said against the latter, in any event it is a harmless form of symbolism; but since it is not a question of real bluebells, we prefer to have them stylized, depicted slightly differently so that they agree with our human idiom of form. We also want to have them incorporated in a sober system, a pattern.

The ancient Egyptians also used plants, bundles of papyrus and lotus, as motives in the shaping of their

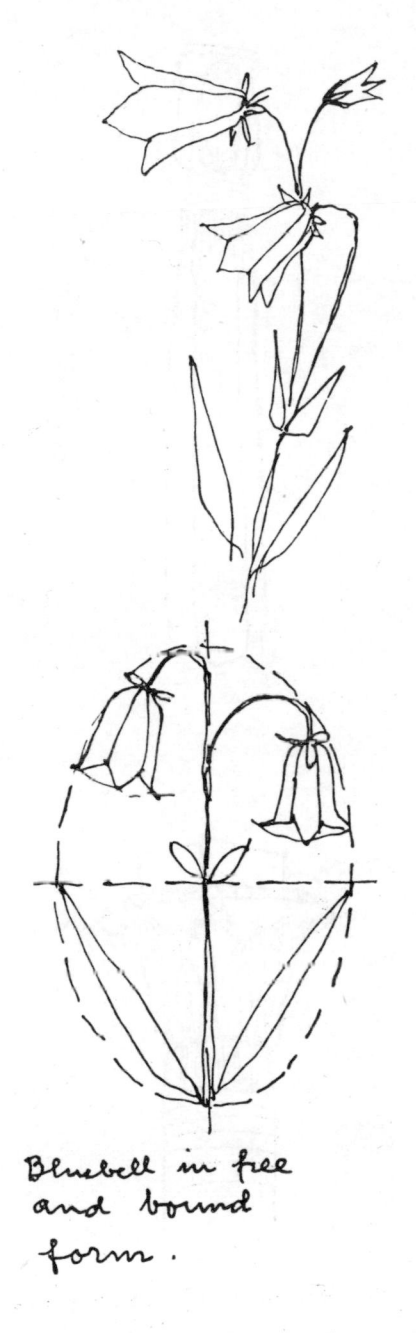

Bluebell in free and bound form.

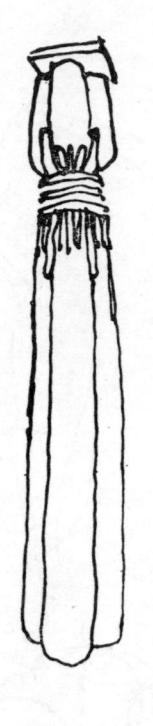

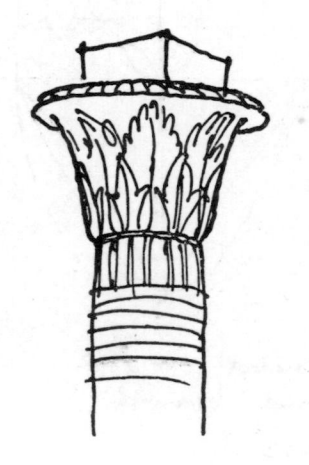

Forms of Egyptian
pillar with plant
motives, strongly
stylized.

pillars. They discovered that things which grew, which stretched straight upwards, provided a natural model for pillars. But they modified the plant-forms so that they were suitable for carving in stone and for their new mission of carrying a heavy roof. (This modification was not entirely successful, as might be expected. A plant is, after all, only meant to carry itself, and the flower at the top has no strength at all of itself.)

What is far more dangerous is when we surround ourselves with forms which remind us of other ages and other ways. We do this partly out of slackness. We "find it so difficult to accustom ourselves to so many new things", although in reality we have already done so completely in other ways. Or else we do so because in our heart of hearts we consider that the old is *finer* and we get a feeling of 'old culture'. Or else we do it because we are fleeing from reality which we find altogether too difficult or unexciting and humdrum. But that again has never been a sensible thing to do.

Many working-class homes provide good examples of this. They attempt to imitate the old upper-middle-class home without having either adequate space or any *real* desire to be like the middle class. It is not mere chance that these examples are of recent date, for the last decade or so has been a time of upheaval in the scientific, economic, political and social spheres. So many new things have happened, and it has all come about at such a speed, that our ability to adjust ourselves has not been able to keep pace. Our heads are jammed with new thoughts and ideas, and this confusion has inevitably had a violent effect on our sense of form, our ability to choose furnishings and furniture which go together.

Imitation of style is not necessarily negative, especially when it is part of the process of maintaining or renewing the ideas of previous ages which are held to be of value.

The whole *Renaissance* was just such a return to the ideals of antiquity. The word itself means rebirth. But such a process presupposes that the situation is otherwise ripe for the idea. The Renaissance, however, was not content just to copy. It also introduced new elements which gave fresh content to the idiom of form.

What is made to act as a reminder can easily also have the stamp of the fake, of being *shoddy*.

QUALITY AND THE SHODDY

We don't mind if a newspaper is printed on thin, bad paper. If it holds together for just a day or two, that is all we ask. But of a book we expect something quite different —we want that to *last*. Or we could express it by saying that the paper ought to be of better *quality*.

This concept of quality, which can thus be translated more or less directly as requirement of durability or suitability for purpose, is one of the best examples of how requirements resulting from practical experience are directly linked with corresponding apprehension of a purely aesthetic kind. Most people will also think that the better paper in the book looks better than the cheap news-print. It is only those used to dealing with problems of form, colour and surface-treatment who are able to disregard this aspect. A painter may suddenly go into raptures about a house which most people regard as an ugly old ruin, because he is only concerned with it as a pictorial impression.

We require different things of the paper in a newspaper and a dictionary.

The notion of quality is not restricted to durability in the absolute sense; it also depends on how the various materials change character under unavoidable wear and tear. A chair made of varnished steel tubing is never so handsome as on the day it emerges new and shining from the factory. Time will crack and chip the varnish, if it does

This would never fetch much in an antique shop.

not make it peel off in flakes. The chair will gradually come to look inferior. But age will, if anything, have the opposite effect on a chair of solid mahogany. Here wear can have an ennobling effect: we think it nice if the hands of generations have set their mark on the arms, making their form soft and pleasant and letting the individual character of the material come into its own. The one may be just as stout as the other, but we undoubtedly think that the quality of the mahogany chair is better.

Similarly, silver and, even more so, gold, are materials of high quality. Compared with other metals they have the excellent quality of not becoming oxidized when in contact with air or water. This special relationship should not lead us into believing that quality is necessarily synonymous with costliness. With us mahogany is more expensive than deal, but even so there is no doubt that the quality of mahogany is the better. It is harder and tougher and more even in substance. In Cuba the relative prices would probably be reversed, yet the qualities would be unchanged. There are, too, a number of things which are coveted just because they are costly, or in other words *rare*. Thus it is quite possible to imagine a rich Cuban wanting to have panelling of Norwegian fir on the walls of his room and thinking that he had thereby acquired something really choice. We must not, however, let such conditions confuse our notions of what quality really is.

The sense of quality is one of the most important qualities to foster if we wish to understand and enjoy the world of things, whether the things are choice and exquisite or the everyday ones of daily life. Thus it is all the more lamentable that just this sense is what we seem to lack most today, and all because of what should otherwise be able to make life better for us in many ways; for example, machine manufacture and mass production, plus the accompanying new materials.

So long as we stuck to natural materials and manufacture by the craftsman or artisan, evaluation of quality was comparatively simple. People had an intuitive understanding of the materials and how they were used. The methods of the craftsman could, of course, use various finesses and secret dodges, but in the main they were based on simple methods which anyone could understand. With machinery this contact disappeared. At the same time, mass production led to materials being used together in combinations which had previously been unheard of, and that further increased the confusion. These new products were cheaper than the old, but to get people really to like them, to think there was something to them, it was desirable to get them to look as like the old, expensive hand-made articles as possible. That is why you find, for example, zinc being painted to look like oak, or iron being pressed so that it has a crinkly surface as though it had been hammered by hand. Such imitations are almost impossible to bring off — so the effect of them is merely confusing, quite apart from the whole thing being pointless. And it becomes quite impossible when what is apparently oak gets scratched and a grey and foreign metal emerges. That reveals the whole thing as being shoddy, and we don't like what is shoddy.

There are countless examples of shoddy fakes which are still being made and which still help to impair our feeling for form: printed cloths with patterns which are meant to look as though they were woven, boards which pretend to be expensive timbers, flimsy leather-cloth which has a surface like that of stout, strong leather, and much else that is rubbishy. But it must also be said that latterly there has been a great improvement here. People have discovered that beauty is no absolute concept in this sphere either, and that you get farther by allowing the materials to look as they are, and that the process of manufacture can make quite new forms entirely natural and give them a new sort of beauty.

At the craftsman's

and in the shop.

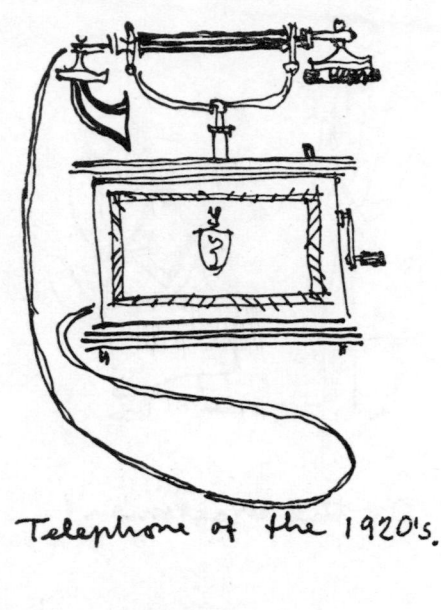

Telephone of the 1920's.

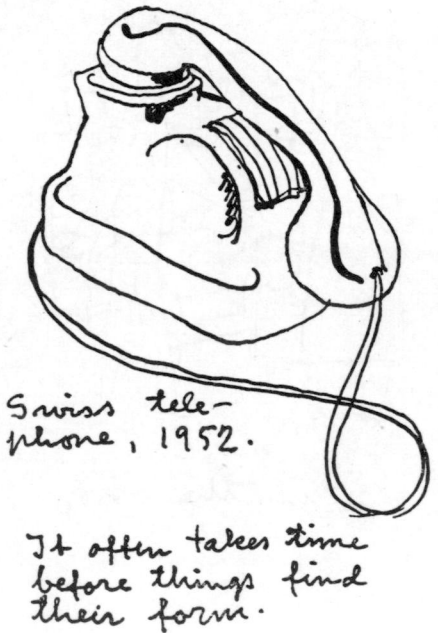

Swiss tele-
phone, 1952.

It often takes time
before things find
their form.

A modern telephone is an excellent example of this process of adaption. It is made of moulded plastic which is excellent for cheap mass production, but which would be quite artificial for a craftsman making things by hand, and this is allowed to act through its own individuality as a compact and thoroughly homogeneous material. Somehow soft round forms 'suit' it best, and these forms also are best suited to the telephone's function. The receiver must lie well in the hand and be pleasant to hold to the ear, and at the same time the inner mechanism must appear to be well protected. Together, the apparatus comprises an entirely new product in respect of which nothing existed to say what form, nature or materials it should have, but only the basic principles. And it has become beautiful.

The telephone isn't perhaps *overwhelmingly* beautiful, but then it is not meant to be. This is a new understanding at which we have slowly arrived in regard to the typical, mass-produced article. It would be intolerable were they to be too special, too intrusive or too personal in their form. Gradually, as we saw them over and over again in every conceivable connection, we should grow thoroughly sick of them. Therefore their beauty must be of a quiet, modest nature which allows them to slip easily and unnoticed into all sorts of contexts without making themselves out to be anything but what they are.

These same ideals of anonymous beauty can be applied to all other kinds of mass product, at any rate those whose origins and mission are quite obvious. A greater and greater proportion of furniture and fittings is coming into this category, which already includes everything we have in the kitchen and bathroom. Our sitting-room furniture may soon follow suit—that is almost no more than a question of economics. To comfort those who dread such a development, we can say that it will give the more personal objects a better chance to shine in their company and also make it economically possible for such things to be there at all.

Finally, we would do well to remember that not absolutely everything has to assume a self-effacing form just because machines have been used to make it. Many machines can be regarded as excellent tools which enable the *craftsman* to work more swiftly or with greater precision, or to execute quite different things from what was possible with his old tools.

Our demand for quality is not confined to the materials, but also applies to the way in which they are treated.

A tumbler which is squint and out of shape and full of bubbles is accounted of poorer quality than one which is smooth and clear and exact in shape, even though the mass is the same. Things should be made properly. That is another requirement which affects our conception of the beautiful. It is a notion of purely aesthetic nature and one which at times can assume an almost religious guise. The materials are regarded as God's gift and we humans ought to show our humble gratitude by treating them with care and veneration. Previously you could find this attitude quite distinctly expressed in certain American Quaker communities, where handicrafts occupied quite an important place. Their slogan was:

"Do your work as though you were going to live for ever and be prepared to die tomorrow."

In other words, take what time you require without niggling, but keep your personal vanity out of it. It is the quality of the product which counts.

Our sense of quality of workmanship has become impaired in the same way as our sense of quality in materials. It looks as though we must find new ways to act in alliance with the new methods of work in restoring an appreciation of these things both in the people who make them and in those who buy them.

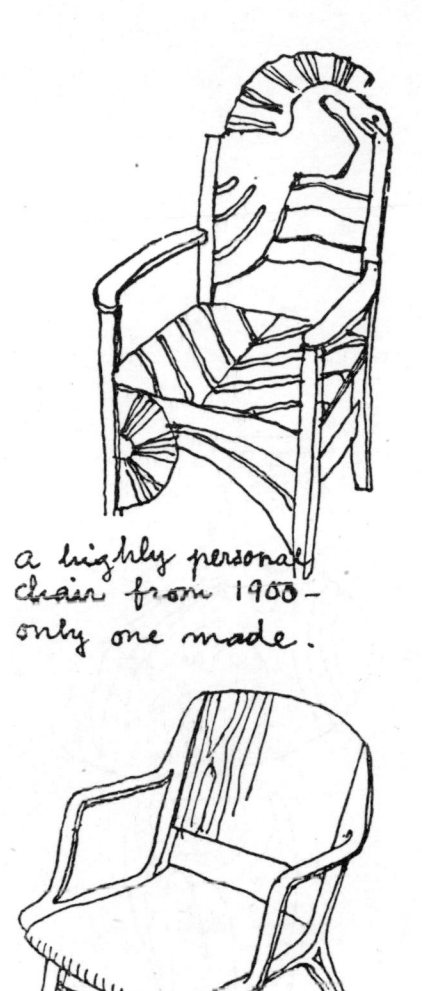

a highly personal chair from 1900 – only one made.

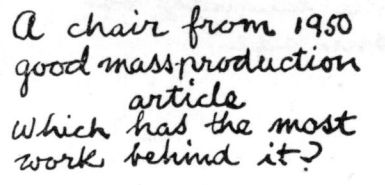

a chair from 1950 good mass-production article which has the most work behind it?

117

CHAPTER TEN

Which deals with our own times and with the things which seem to determine our sense of form.

It is quite impossible to make such an analysis of our own age as would satisfactorily explain the background of our experiences in the sphere of form. We can see too little of the picture for that; there are too many factors for them to be classified and arranged. But perhaps we could discover some main features, things which make our age more or less different from those which preceded it and which have had a decisive influence on our world of ideas.

We have several times used the word 'development' as though it were a well-known and concrete phenomenon. We all, of course, realize that a lot of things have happened in the last hundred years. It is perhaps debatable whether they have also meant development in the sense of having led to something better; but at any rate they have brought about a number of changes to which we must try to conform if we are to be able to get any cohesion and order in the picture. Without this sense of cohesion we cannot live comfortably. We will try here to summarize the changes which are of interest to us and arrange them in three groups which we shall call New Knowledge, New Requirements, New Impressions.

NEW KNOWLEDGE

Externally, our age is characterized by the enormous advances made in the domains of technics and the natural

Picasso ceramic 1950. The language of our age?

118

sciences. It would be possible to make long lists of technical productions, but it will be enough here to mention a few individual examples which obviously affect our daily lives. The most obvious are the *motor-car* and the *aeroplane*, and though we may not all own or use such means of transport, they both have an established place in our consciousness. They also provide the bulk of modern children's toys. But there are others we can mention, more unpretentious, like the telephone or, to stick to the kitchen regions, the mix-master and the pressure cooker. Drawing lamps, radiators and washing machines also come into that category.

All these are tools which we hold in honour and esteem because they render us more efficient at the same time as they make our daily lives more pleasant in a variety of ways. They are not mere insignificant aids, but very much objects of our attention. That is to say that their forms are also objects of our attention. Architects and designers put a lot of work into getting them good and right, and, con-versely, the man in the street will be strongly influenced by the appearance given to these things because he is so closely associated with them.

By virtue of the nature of things these forms will be of an entirely technical-functional kind, and that allows us to say straight away that the feeling of beauty attaching to the good and perfect tool must of necessity assume a dominant position in the consciousness of our age. It will as a matter of course receive expression in the examples mentioned here, but it will also infect other things which are by no means so technical in origin. For we happen to be so made that we all try to comprehend our ideals of form as best we can.

A special example of what this involves is the *stream-lined form*, which is the form a body ought to have if the resistance of the air is to be as small as possible. This form is thus desirable for everything which has to move at great

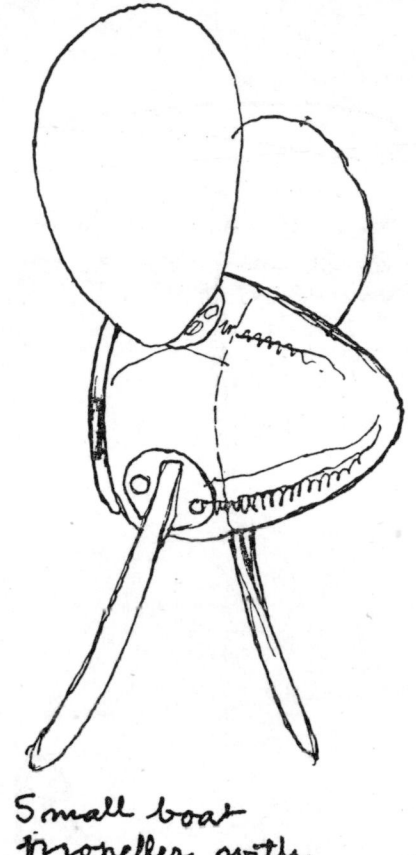

Small boat propeller with fine, rich forms.

119

The streamline form as it can appear in an aeroplane. —

— and when imitated in a pram.

speed and it has therefore been scientifically investigated in connection with flying technique. Here we have got an entirely new form to work with, and it has also acquired content and meaning for us, quite spontaneously, thanks to our new knowledge about these things. To people from the age of rococo it would appear meaningless or ugly.

It was also natural to give an, at any rate, approximately stream-lined form to the body of the motor-car. Since both motor-car and aeroplanes are popular things, the stream-lined form has also become popular. People think it is intrinsically elegant. The result has been its adoption for a number of other articles such as irons, wirelesses and prams, where it does not belong. We can say that we have to do here with a *style-forming* factor, which is itself an amusing thing to note, but it can easily come to look in the wrong place because of its highly specialized background.

Medical science is another of the spheres where developments have been swift in our own day. The new knowledge which has thereby come to the man in the street, and which is also of interest to us, is the understanding of hygiene, both physical and mental. The whole concept of *health* has been given a new place in our world of ideas. Translated into the idiom of the world of form, this means that amongst other things we dress with an eye to health and mobility, or to put it more simply in other words, without fuss or frippery. We also arrange our homes to a considerable extent so that they may be easy to keep clean, especially in the kitchen and bathroom. Also when we choose such things as material for curtains and covers, or the number of panes in the windows or of panels for the doors, we do so with a thought as to whether it will be easy to keep clean.

It is perhaps wrong to say that considerations of this kind really dominate our ideas of the nature of things—and we have, after all, also got new aids for getting rid of what dust and dirt may accumulate. With a vacuum cleaner we can keep plush upholstery as sanitary as if it had been linen. But if we walked into a school classroom where there were plush covers on the seats of the desks and a thick carpet on the floor, our reaction would be instantaneous. And it would not be the unnecessary expense at which we would protest, but at the difficulties of keeping the place clean. It has been said that the modern way of furnishing rooms and style of furniture have made their way into people's consciousness through the bath. That is rather one-sided, but not without justification.

Our appreciation of *mental* hygiene has lead first and foremost to the recognition that each individual needs to be able to be by himself – at any rate on occasion – to be able to go into his room and shut the door behind him and relax without others seeing and controlling. This need has had a decisive effect on the design of houses and flats which have become progressively more differentiated and split-up. We must also assume that sense of form is affected by new insights into these purely psychic phenomena, even though it would be difficult to show how. But, to return to the classroom, if we say that lines ought to be restful and room forms also, colours soft and quiet, everyone will understand why. We also use the expression 'quiet' in a commendatory way when talking of the impression a room gives, so that there is evidently some association of ideas here. A typical result of our interest in these things is the way we want to discover how different colours and forms quite spontaneously affect the mind. This has become an entirely new field of research, and indeed this whole book is an illustration of the tendency.

a well-shaped apparatus like this must of necessity also have affected our sense of form.

NEW REQUIREMENTS

So far we have only mentioned examples of how new science has directly affected our external world. The

American chair, designed for mass-production. The "cheap forms" have acquired their own attraction.

indirect effects, however, are even more decisive. These amount to a tremendous upheaval of social relationships, a displacement and development in the social sphere which makes our position utterly different from that of our grandfathers.

Now that more and more of all productive work is being done with the help of machines, it has been possible to shorten the working day. And since machinery produces things cheaply, it has been possible to increase wage-rates for those who look after them, and these two circumstances have together led to a levelling of the differences between the various strata of society. We could also say that the *standard of living*, that is, the clothing, food, dwellings and furniture we all have, has been considerably improved.

Or we can also say that things have become relatively *cheaper*. But since our prosperity is based on this cheapness, this quality of cheapness has simultaneously become an ideal. If we exaggerate slightly, we can say that we like certain things *because* they are cheap, provided they are decent as well. In other ages it has been the other way round: things have been considered beautiful just because they were very expensive. It all depends on what the criterion is. But we must also remember that what is required of the individual has also increased with the standard of living. The law requires that we all go to school for ten years at least; but this does not merely involve our presence in school during certain hours, but also necessitates the provision of a place in our homes where we can do our prep. and work in peace.

In most countries all adults have the right to vote and elect people to represent them in parliament. That is an excellent thing, but it is pointless unless those who vote are able to follow things sufficiently to know what it is they are voting about.

We must also assume that the jobs people have to do

today, on the whole, are much more complicated, exacting and wearing than they were a mere hundred years ago. This does not apply only to the adult world. We also want our children to show interest in a multitude of things, to be occupied with many different hobbies. We let them become scouts, play in bands, learn dancing and attend all sorts of courses, hoping that it will fit them eventually to enter the world of the adults.

All this must of necessity give us a sense for what is *effective*, what is serviceable, what will help us to attain a given result. Where things are concerned, this means that we tend to concentrate on their importance as tools. We think of how they can help us, increase our efficiency, on the one hand, and our rightful claim for leisure on the other. That is why we prefer to give things the form which will make them most usable, and this would not be possible were we to give most consideration to purely formal ideals of form. Our functionalistic attitude can to that extent be said to be a *style-destructive* element. Many will consider the result pretty devoid of feeling, but we must remember what was said earlier about love of things as tools. That can be a deep, warm love and a thoroughly sound and healthy one.

We must be able to keep up with things.

NEW IMPRESSIONS

Today most people have a newspaper thrust through their door every morning. In it they can read about war, death and destruction, and perhaps see a picture of a child picking the first primrose. There are reviews of books and criticisms of plays, reports of new fashions, and a whole lot of other things. Thus even the first hour of the day begins with an overwhelming confusion of *impressions*. And even though we may not read the paper very thoroughly, its very presence reminds us that great and important things are taking place up and down the world, and that there are a

We are overwhelmed
by impressions.

lot of people busied with a lot of problems about which they wish to inform others.

And so it goes on all day. On the way to school or where we work, we move in a stream of impressions, especially if our way leads through the streets of a city. We may see a new car model; an excavator with its peculiar claws; posters and placards; to say nothing of a stream of strange people. When we return home in the afternoon, we switch on the wireless and fill our heads with music, weather reports, talks about things we don't rightly understand, and still more news. Perhaps we end the day with a book, preferably an exciting one, or we go to the cinema. And there in the dark, we are translated to completely different surroundings with entirely different kinds of people, occupied with other things altogether than those which make up our own existence. And even though we have been able to get through the swarm of the day's impressions more or less unaffected, here we have to give up. In a series of close-ups and cunning shots the producer imprints upon our retinas pictures of water fronts, beautiful women, gun-play and strange wild beasts.

And along with all this are the deep impressions of the primal things, of snow falling on a calm winter's day, of the hiss of a fir wood in a shower of rain, of the flight of swallows and the rhythm of the waves.

If we could imagine a monk of the Middle Ages being suddenly translated into our world of today, the probability is that he would go out of his mind, for to be able to support such a strain calls for a long process of adjustment. This consists of our learning to defend ourselves against the multiplicity of impressions, of our minds becoming hardened.

We must assume that there is a definite limit to how much a normal person can feel, perceive or apprehend. A man who lives in the country among Nature will have an eye for the form of leaves and flowers, for the passage of clouds and

124

the play of wind in the tree-tops. From these he will be able to read the shifts and changes in weather and the seasons, of the eternal mystery of life. A man who lives in a garden city is to a certain extent surrounded by the same things, but they will not tell him so much. That is, he will not apprehend it all, for he will have so many other impressions with which he will also have to deal.

This line of thought leads to the conclusion that the ability to interpret the impressions *things* make on us, will diminish progressively as our world becomes surfeited with such impressions. Theirs is the quietest voice of all and we must have both time and an open mind if we are to catch them. And that is most regrettable, for it is not on the number of experiences, but on their nature and composition, that depends whether or not the total picture is harmonious. Thus we ought partly to try to increase the attention we give to these things, but also partly to accept the situation. Such an attitude is more or less identical with what we said earlier when discussing the wisdom of letting a number of articles of daily necessity have a modest, anonymous place in our form-world, and focusing our interest on the individual, choice things. We should also remember that the *whole* can be just as decisive as the individual object.

It is possible to imagine a room where neither chairs, table, door nor windows give us any form of experience when taken individually, yet the arrangement, their mutual cohesion, together with their colours and texture gives a rich picture full of experience.

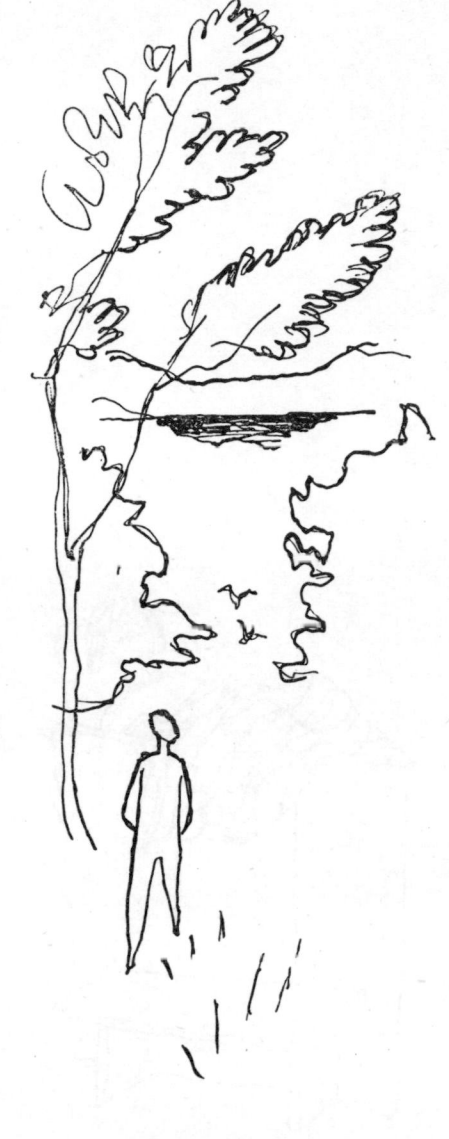

CURTAIN SPEECH

All the special features of our age which we have mentioned here seem to point, as far as the idiom of form is concerned, in one distinct direction: that where our choice is free, we prefer the simple, quiet forms, and that in the

We will always hear the voice of Nature.

first place we have an eye to their value as articles of use, that is to say, the forms which reflect the services the things render us.

Many people perhaps will say that this means that we have reached a state in which there are no possibilities for development, that the forms of the various articles will be fixed once and for all as soon as we know sufficient about their use to be able to make them absolutely 'right'. There are, however, no grounds for such a fear, for the manner of using things will keep on changing and with it the determinant for their form. Everything is liable to alteration in this way, even the way people lie and sleep in a bed can change from one age to another as the picture in the margin shows.

The functionalistic way of reasoning must not be taken as a dry and ossified idea. On the contrary, a good tool has the power to increase our performance; it increases our ability to develop, even to develop our lives. Therefore such an attitude and the forms in which it is represented will always contain within themselves the possibility of development.

It is *here* that we can rightly demand something more, something which will release imagination, which has really no other purpose than to delight and enrich. Or something which, so to speak, pulls everything together, so that our performance is always stamped by what is our common attitude, the normal for our upbringing and way of thinking. We can develop on one side the free, individual performance or we can accentuate; on the other side the governing idea of the form.

But in all circumstances we must learn to watch our things, to form them with care, to *cultivate* them. Cultivate really means to till the ground, an action which makes us richer. And so we use the word metaphorically of the work which we perform in order to be able to feel richer mentally.

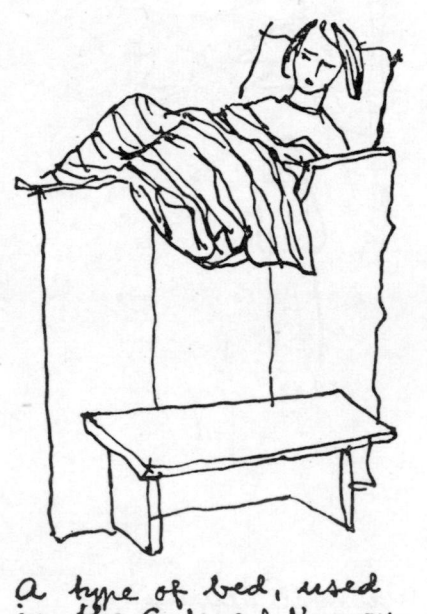

A type of bed, used in the Setesdal, Norway. Everything can change, even the way we sleep.

126

le Corbusier. Rich interplay of simple forms.

Everybody has the ability to perform such work, every-one has an urge to form and shape, and everybody is also equipped with a certain amount of creative imagination. It is these abilities and gifts we must watch over for the delight of the individual and us all.

Look how freely and uninhibitedly children get to work when they get hold of a box of paints or something to model with—there isn't anything which gives them greater joy. What they make isn't always so very correct as far as accurate rendering of reality is concerned, but to make up for that they have an intuitive ability to find expression for what seems to them to be the essential and vital aspect of things. They use such colours and forms as they feel inclined to use without thought of whether they are correct, or whether they are beautiful or not. But they must tally with something or other.

Extravagance often goes well with unpretentious peasant art. It comprises a little of everything.

These are abilities which we all had once and which we should try to dig out again. But we mustn't behave *merely* like children. We must also apply what we have learned in the meantime and use it both to find new expressions and to comprise, arrange and cultivate the whole. If we can manage to do that our form-world will also become *right,* in the sense that it will reflect in a harmonious way both our inner and external worlds, comprising and deepening at one and the same time. And then, too, we shall have a greater chance of ourselves being in harmony, which will give pleasure both to us and all with whom we live.